revisionaries
A DECADE OF ART IN TOKION

revisionaries
A DECADE OF ART IN TOKION

abrams image
new york

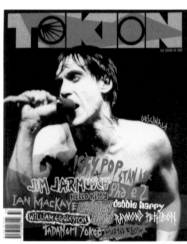

[this page and facing page, clockwise from top left]
magazine cover art by Brent Rollins, Ryan McGinley, Jimmy Turrell, Kim Hiorthøy, Cristophe Rihet, Noah Butkus, Nagi Noda, Deanne Cheuk with Andre Weismayr, Deanne Cheuk

Tokion editor: Ken Miller
Abrams Image: Eva Prinz with Sofia Gutierrez
Design: Neil Egan
Production managers: Anet Sirna-Bruder and Jacquie Poirier
Thanks to: Abbye Churchill, Melissa Seley, and Maxwell Williams

Cataloging-in-publication data has been applied for and is available from the Library of Congress.

ISBN 13: 978-0-8109-9437-9
ISBN 10: 0-8109-9437-2

Printed and bound in China
10 9 8 7 6 5 4 3 2 1

HNA ▪▪▪▪▪
harry n. abrams, inc.
a subsidiary of La Martinière Groupe
115 West 18th Street
New York, NY 10011
www.hnabooks.com

[right, top to bottom] T-shirt artwork by David Ellis, Brian Degraw, Deanne Cheuk, Noah Butkus, and Tomoo Gokita

I spent a few years in art school in the early '90s, back when the '80s aesthetic still defined the tone. The art they were teaching at school didn't exactly speak to me. I came to believe that the "art world" and I didn't have a future together, so I dropped out. For me, the work that resonated most wasn't on the gallery walls or in the classroom slideshows, but in between the covers of underground comic books, on the bottoms of skateboard decks, and printed across punk rock T-shirts.

From there, I searched curiously for culture that appealed to my personal interests. I found a group of young creatives bubbling up from the subways and skate parks and DJ booths. They were my age and they created art that I "got." I knew I wanted to be a part of that energy. This was how *Tokion* magazine began.

That was ten years ago. At that time, outside of one or two independent galleries and a few Japanese street-wear companies, there were no real platforms provided to showcase this new, loosely formed group of young talent. So we got to work providing it through *Tokion*. We collaborated with this community to make T-shirts, stickers, posters, short films, and just generally spread the word. There was no real money to be made and only a small number of people were interested or aware.

Slowly the art world began to catch up to these sensibilities, and the group of artists represented in *Tokion*, and in this book, have now all grown up. *Tokion* grew alongside them, from a fifty-six-page two-color 'zine to a glossy, internationally distributed title.

For kids entering the art world today, there now exists a flourishing support system of independent magazines, young galleries, marketing companies, the Internet, and a white-hot art market that wasn't around ten years ago. And that initial lack of interest in "the alternative" probably turned out to be a blessing in disguise for many artists, providing a few years of gestation when their work was basically seen only by peers, allowing it to mature and grow properly. I remember that time fondly, and believe it was that initial burst of energy that still fuels interest in the art on these pages.

I sometimes wonder how the art and culture covered in the early issues of *Tokion* managed to bubble up from the bottom to resonate on a larger scale, and I believe the answer is simply authenticity. In an era when culture is quickly co-opted by marketing, and the images that surround us are increasingly conformed, actual sincerity is pleasing to the eye. True folk art is becoming obsolete, falling victim to mass production and technology, but its spirit continues in new ways. The break beat has replaced the banjo; T-shirt graphics have replaced sign painters; blogs are the new after-dinner storytelling, and so on.

The art of *Revisionaries* is the folk art of the twenty-first century. And if its unrefined origins and influences bar it from art school curriculums, that's probably a blessing in disguise. This work is available to be discovered by new fans based solely on its merits . . . Just like *Tokion*.

Adam Glickman
Founder

[above] cover artwork by Kevin Lyons

[from left] artwork by Barry McGee, Margaret Kilgallen, Barry McGee, Os Gemeos (photo by Souris Hong-Porretta). *Tokion* product photography by Mariah Robertson

When I started working at *Tokion*, I don't think I realized I was going to be editing an art magazine. It looked great. It had art in it. But if it didn't engage in endless discussions of what was going on in the art world, didn't analyze trends and purchase prices, and most of all, didn't aggressively editorialize about art, then it couldn't really be an art magazine, could it? The possibility of art being discussed as part of a larger mix of culture had, for me, become an almost forgotten idea.

So it's perhaps a bit odd and surprising that, after a decade of making *Tokion*, we decided that the best way to summarize what has excited us about the magazine was to gather together the artists who have been featured in or collaborated with or just somehow been friendly with the magazine. And even with ninety artists included, *Revisionaries* is by no means a complete collection of everyone who has helped out or inspired the magazine over the years. Unfortunately we don't have enough time or paper to make that book.

The common bond among all of the artists you see here is that we have found their work inspiring and amazing in some way. And a big part of what has inspired us about these artists is that they haven't been afraid to break down that invisible barrier between art and the rest of society's cultural output. One of the most frustrating aspects of my job while editing *Tokion* was to constantly have to refer to it as an "art and culture" magazine, as if the two were somehow different.

Within the pages of the magazine, we felt pretty comfortable throwing music, film, fashion, design, and other random cultural detritus together in a big heap, leaving it to the reader to sort through the mix to find their particular source of inspiration. Outside the pages of the magazine, more often than not the universes of art and culture seem to exist completely separately—parallel, but never touching. But not so long ago, a small number of artists were actual celebrities, and it was conceivable that you would see Keith Haring, Jeff Koons, Andy Warhol, or Jean-Michel Basquiat being interviewed on a talk show, courting the mainstream by speaking its language. They were in an ongoing dialogue with the rest of the culture, and if their art was, as often as not, quite pop, they in turn were pop stars.

Because of this they had an impact on an audience that ranged beyond art school kids and avid collectors. By disregarding the boundaries of the art world, they went on to influence the culture at large (in particular, the visual culture), and they certainly affected my worldview, aesthetics, and sense of identity while I was growing up. Did it really matter if the Keith Haring "Crack Is Wack" sculpture near my high school was "street art" or fine art? Would the Raymond Pettibon piece on the cover of Sonic Youth's *Goo* have been any less a work of art if it had appeared on the album first? What was important was that I found them, or they found me, an opening of my eyes that eventually led me to become the editor in chief of *Tokion*.

What is exciting about the artists in *Revisionaries* is that they show how unimportant genre distinctions and art world exclusivity are. They reflect influences and styles ranging from street art to punk show flyers to skate graphics to video game design to stoned doodling, and they're using devalued media such as collage, drawing, and video art, all to maximum graphic impact. In so doing, they're reflecting their influences back to the viewer, and they're actually reengaging with the world around them. Yes, you still need a gallery to sell your work to collectors (unless you make your living as a graphic artist), but an album cover, magazine article, or web page can make you an art star to a far bigger audience that until recently felt excluded from the art world.

Through the influence of this younger generation of artists, what had until very recently felt like an elite, insular art community has begun to open up to a wider audience. And as it opens to a wider audience, you can start to see art scenes and communities pop up in places that are far removed from the gallery network. *Tokion* certainly didn't start this development, but it has been exciting, over the past few years, to be able to be a part of this rapidly growing scene. In a lot of ways, it reminds me of what happened to the music industry in the 1990s, when "underground" indie rock, dance music, and hip-hop suddenly stormed the mainstream. You still needed a major label to get on the radio, but within a few short years, the number of independent record labels exploded, opening up outlets for regional music communities and obscure styles.

Over the past few years the number of galleries and artists showing in them has increased, seemingly exponentially. Within the U.S., regional scenes have blossomed and gained prominence. And in the same way that music critics used to talk about the Minneapolis, Athens, or Chapel Hill sounds, art fans now discuss the output of art scenes in Providence, Miami, Chicago, Philadelphia, San Francisco, and Los Angeles. And thanks to the Internet, these networks stretch internationally as well.

Perhaps due to this ease of access, this new art is very home-grown and do-it-yourself. And that is the big difference I see between the artists gathered in this book and those big names I mentioned earlier. When the celebrity artists of my youth dealt with pop culture, they still did so from an elite "art world" perspective. So when Andy Warhol talked about everyone getting their fifteen minutes of fame, I think he still fancied himself playing a part in deciding who and when. He did create his own "stars," after all.

Today, mass culture moves so quickly that styles develop, bubble up from the various (numerous) undergrounds, become co-opted and marketed, and then get recycled and quoted, all within the span of a few web pages. And in this increasingly rapid and free-form dialogue, these artists aren't just commenting on culture, but engaging with it. It's time for those parallel universes to officially meet. They'll both be better for it.

Ken Miller
Editor in Chief, 2002–2007

ANTHONY YANKOVIC FAILE

ANDREW KUO

GEOFF McFETRIDGE

BRENTROLLINS

CHRISTINA VANTZOU

JOSH PETHERICK

CHUCK ANDERSON

SHEPARD FAIREY

DALEK JULIE VERHOEVEN

DAVID ELLIS RYAN McGINNESS

ELISABETH ARKHIPOFF

JOSE PARLA

JON SANTOS

ROSTARR

KIM HIORTHOY

SUN AN

MAYA HAYUK

SAIMAN CHOW

MIKE MILLS

JIMMY TURRELL

NOAH BUTKUS

JESSE ALEXANDER

NAGI NODA

SWOON

PERKS AND MINI

ANDREW KUO

Born: New York City
Lives: New York City

When was the first time you exhibited your art in public?
I guess the first time was in Providence, where I went to college. At the end of your senior year, they put on a show of some people's stuff. I showed a billboard-sized photo of myself in war paint and a giant bone. I was really into that kind of stuff back then. I've mellowed since, but sometimes I wish I hadn't.

What was that experience like?
I wish I could say more about that specific show. It was just whatever. My first proper "solo" was terrifying, though. And frustrating, satisfying, inspiring, etc. They all become this one big messy thing.

What is one lesson you've learned since then?
That a show is not a big deal in the way you think it is. And it's a huge deal in another way . . . As an action that leads to another step in your art "making" career, but not your art "recognition" career, which matters less and less as you make more work.

How would you say your relationship to your work has evolved since that time?
I think that as you get older you either become

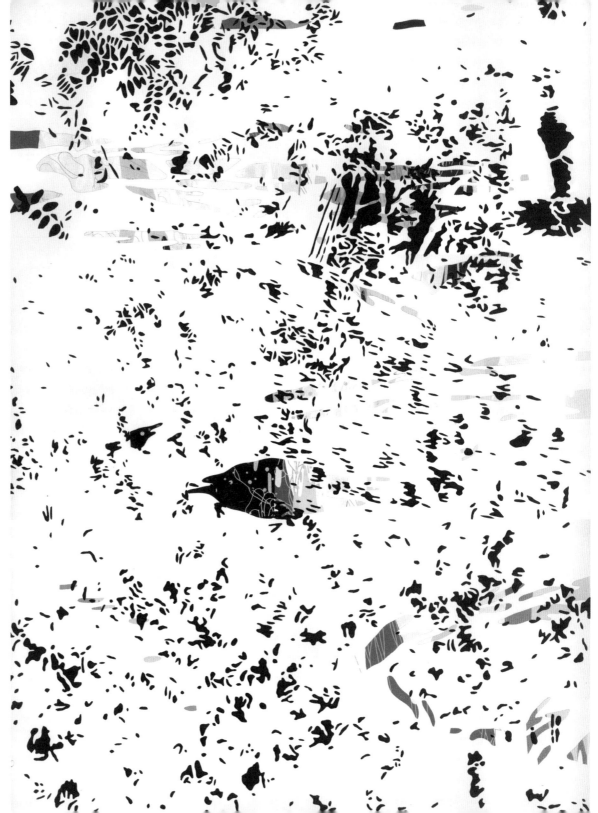

more involved in your work, or you don't. I've become more involved in it in a lot of ways.

What is the nicest compliment you've received about your work?
Two of my friends who lived in the same apartment both bought huge paintings from me at the same time at my first NYC show . . . How nice was that?

What is the most frustrating thing to hear about your work?
"You are a graphic artist." I mean, isn't every artist graphic?

If you could change one thing about how you make and exhibit work, what would it be?
I guess I wish my work was better. Doesn't every artist want to be the best ever?

[from left to right]

It's Getting Late
2006
acrylic ink and paint on paper
14 × 20 in.

I've Always Liked You, But Whatever
2005
acrylic ink and paint on paper
14 × 20 in.

You Don't Know What You're Missing
2006
acrylic ink and paint on paper
14 × 20 in.

ANTHONY YANKOVIC

Born: Cleveland, OH
Lives: St. Petersburg, FL

When was the first time you exhibited your art in public?
What was that experience like?
May 2001. It was a two-man show, back in
my student days. Overall, it was a rewarding
experience, for being a small exhibition in the
middle of southern Ohio.

What is one lesson you've learned since that time?
Don't expect to blow minds unless you've really
created something mind-blowing.

How would you say your relationship to your work has
evolved since that time?
I try not to overdo it anymore. In the past, I've
had the tendency to make every piece look like
it took a million man-hours to produce. Which
is a ridiculous way to design, paint or illustrate
anything in good taste. Just cramming the
canvas with a bunch of razzle-dazzle or dingle-
dangles won't win any awards. The simplest
solution is usually the best . . . sometimes.

Who do you consider to be your peers?
Maybe it's to my detriment, but I lead a solitary
existence in terms of sharing my work.

What is the nicest compliment you've received about
your work?
"Can I buy that?"

What is the most frustrating thing to hear about
your work?
"There's too much going on."

If you could change one thing about how you make and
exhibit work, what would it be?
Finding a cheaper way to frame works on paper.

How do you discover most artists you like?
The library. I tend to look to the past more than
the future for inspiration.

[from left to right]

To Your Health
2006
mixed media
11 × 17 in.

Taking Maniac Pills
2006
mixed media
18 × 24 in.

Bastardly Deeds
2006
mixed media
11 × 17 in.

BRENT ROLLINS

Born: Los Angeles, CA
Lives: New York City

When was the first time you exhibited your art in public?
In 1997, I think, at a defunct nightclub in the West Village called LIFE. It was a group show.

What was that experience like?
It was exciting because it was an ambition of mine to show in an NYC art show. Also, it was frustrating because it was an opportunity that came during a time when my abilities were less developed. Ultimately, it was relieving, because I think ideas are made to be shared with the public.

What is one lesson you've learned since that time?
The act and the result are of equal value.

How would you say your relationship to your work has evolved since that time?
I allow myself to explore ideas and processes and make mistakes. I'm very confident in my ability.

What is the most frustrating thing to hear about your work?
I guess it would be the suggestion that I'm not a "real" artist because I work primarily in a digital realm. Yeah, there's value and craft to any hand-produced process, but the expression of the idea is what is fundamental. The medium or process shouldn't be exclusive in defining what an artist is. That's a snobby attitude to take.

If you could change one thing about how you make and exhibit work, what would it be?
I need an easier, cheaper method to produce more work! The creation phase is cheap but time consuming. Transferring it from digital form to an interesting medium is the challenge and expense.

What is one emerging artist whose work you find exciting or intriguing?
To quote Andy Warhol, "All of them."

How useful do you think a magazine like *Tokion* can be for an artist?
Recognition anywhere is valuable, but magazines like *Tokion* are essential and influential arbiters of taste for this global-centric generation. It's definitely helped cultivate the current state of popular art appreciation. With the passive nature and insular network of the gallery world, it's likely that an artist's exposure in *Tokion* can influence the galleries. I'm sure many artists who exhibit outside of their hometowns have been contacted simply because someone at

such-and-such gallery saw an article about them in a magazine. Not saying the gallery is lazy, but it is a static entity. It's not as populist and transient by nature as a publication is. For some, a gallery offers a prestige factor and an environment where, at best, their work can be viewed with maximum one-on-one impact. But if you care that your work is seen by the greatest number of people, there's no reason not to share via public art or via publication.

Skyborn
2001
digital collage, spray enamel
20 × 40 in.

SCLA
2006
digital photography and collage
20 × 40 in.

15

CHRISTINA VANTZOU

Born: Kansas City, MO
Lives: Brussels, Belgium

When was the first time you exhibited your art in public?
My mom is an artist and she organized regular art openings at my parents' restaurant. My favorite one growing up was the annual Valentine's group show.

What is one lesson you've learned since that time?
A little organization goes a long way. Progress is slow. Sometimes it takes a while before you can tell if something is any good. The less you care about making a good drawing, the better you draw. It's all part of letting go. Easy is OK, but cutting corners shows in the end. Invest in a good chair.

What is the nicest compliment you've received about your work?
A compliment on my color choices usually goes a long way. I am very picky about colors, and I spend an awful lot of time and money at the art-supply store, testing all the markers.

If you could change one thing about how you make and exhibit work, what would it be?
I feel like I'm working on a giant, never-ending puzzle. Lately, I've been working on daily studio maintenance and correcting bad habits, such as leaving things half finished. I also notice an unnecessary amount of stress managing my projects. It's a mental thing, self-generated, so thinking less would be a nice change.

[from left to right]

Blue Stretch on Old Paper
2006
ink, marker, and Photoshop on found paper
8.25 × 11 in.

Japanese Garden with scribbles
2006
ink and marker on paper
11.8 × 17 in.

CHUCK ANDERSON

Born: Lancaster, PA
Lives: Tinley Park, IL

When was the first time you exhibited your art in public?
The first time I really ever exhibited my work in public was also the first time I'd ever done public speaking. It was in New York City, at Lincoln Center, in September 2005, for the show "Semi-Permanent."

I was in front of over a thousand people with my work on full display behind me on two screens for a full hour. That was nerve wracking, because I was actually there with the work and not just an anonymous name behind a screen anymore.

What is one lesson you've learned since that time? I've learned to develop a thick skin to people who make uneducated or rude comments, but also to learn the fine line between that and constructive criticism and friendly suggestion.

I've also become a much better public speaker. That first time was quite a learning experience.

How would you say your relationship to your work has evolved since that time?
I've developed techniques and methods for certain things, but also have learned how to try new things I've never done before. I like finishing working on something and saying to myself, "Wow, I learned something new that time."

What is the nicest compliment you've received about your work?
Anytime a student e-mails me that I've inspired them to pursue a career in art or design. That is a pretty awesome feeling, to hear that I've affected someone's life in that way.

What is the most frustrating thing to hear about your work?
That I just do the same thing over and over again. I really disagree, because even something that looks a little like what came before probably had something in it that was new for me to try. I also get sick of hearing people assume they know how I create my work and how easy it is. If it was really that easy there would be more people doing it.

[from left to right]

Humanlike
2006
photography and digitally colored art, matte print
20 × 16 in.

Good Parts of Bad Dreams
2006
photography and digitally colored art, matte print
18 × 24 in.

DALEK

Born: New London, CT
Lives: New York City

When was the first time you exhibited your art in public?
For a seventh-grade school art show I made a papier mâché dragon. It was at the height of D&D mania. The next time after that was in 1996 at a group show Modart put on at the ASR trade show in San Diego. Shepard Fairey and Mike Nelson helped hook me up with that.

What was that experience like?
Pretty inspiring. There is certainly something amazing about having something you create be displayed in a public context, especially when it is surrounded by the work of other folks you admire.

What is one lesson you've learned since that time?
Not to place expectations on anything.

How would you say your relationship to your work has evolved since that time?
It changes and evolves all the time. I think a lot of it is a subconscious output as my life changes and as my technical abilities grow stronger from repetition.

What is the most frustrating thing to hear about your work?
When folks don't believe they are painted, and believe they are printed or something. I've had folks tell me I am straight up lying to them.

[from left to right]

Untitled (detail)
2006
acrylic on wood panel
24 × 24 in.

Untitled
2007
acrylic on wood panel
36 × 36 in.

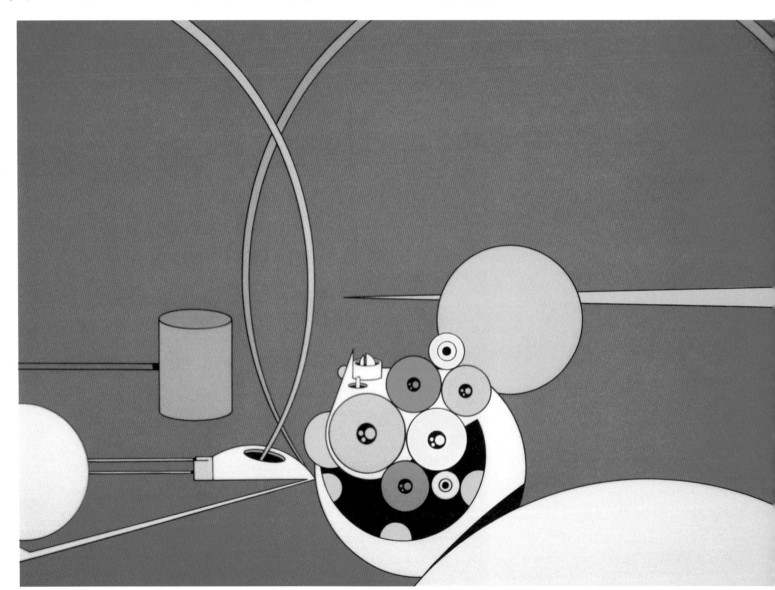

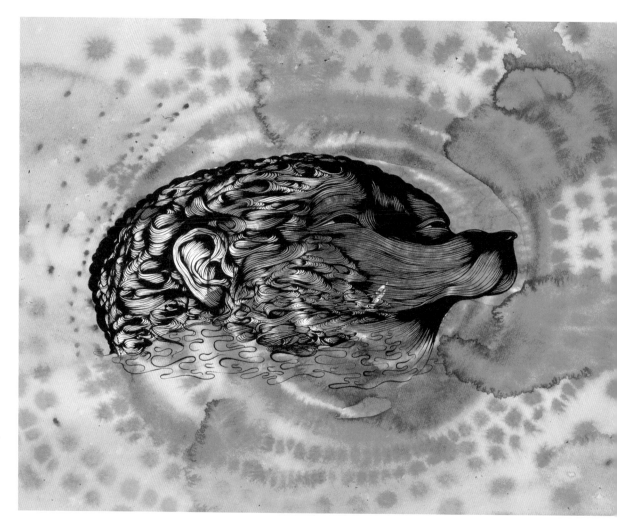

DAVID ELLIS

Born: North Carolina
Lives: New York City

When was the first time you exhibited your art in public?
I started painting graffiti on tobacco barns and
chicken houses in 1983.

If you could change one thing about how you make and
exhibit work, what would it be?
Less time on the computer.

[from left to right]

Dog Grouse
2004
ink and tobacco stain on watercolor paper
30 × 25 in.

Snake 1200 Versions 1 And 2
2003
ink and tobacco stain on watercolor paper
30 × 25 in.

Catfish
2004
ink and tobacco stain on watercolor paper
30 × 25 in.

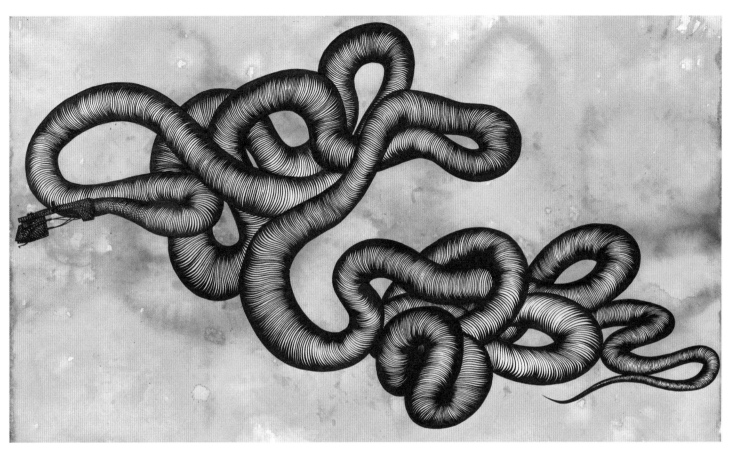

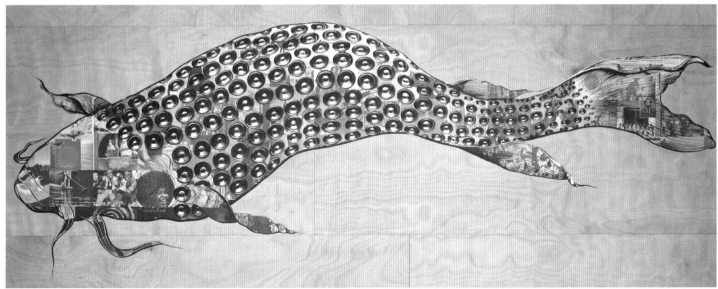

ELISABETH
ARKHIPOFF

born: Abidjan, Ivory Coast
lives: New York City

When was the first time you exhibited your art in public?
In 2000, at the Paris Museum of Modern Art.

What is one lesson you've learned since that time?
Work within a budget!

[from left to right]

Untitled (part of the "1978, 1983?" series)
2002
mixed media collage on book

Swarovski fashion campaign
2006-2007
mixed media collage on paper
9 × 9 in.

FAILE

Patrick McNeil
Born: Edmonton, Canada
Lives: New York City

Patrick Miller
Born: Minneapolis, MN
Lives: New York City

Aiko Nakagawa
Born: Tokyo, Japan
Lives: New York City

When was the first time you exhibited your art in public?
On the street in New York City in 1998.

What is the nicest compliment you've received about your work?
Just that it's really inspired people to create and make work of their own. It's amazing to see the cycle of people that inspire you to create and then to have that affect on someone else—passing it on, in a sense.

What is the most frustrating thing to hear about your work?
"Are you going to take that shit off my building?"

As far as you know, how have most people discovered your work, or what has gotten you the most attention?
Definitely putting work up on the street. This in turn is photographed and published in books or magazines or posted on the web. From there the exposure seems to grow exponentially.

[from left to right]

It Happens Everyday
2007
acrylic and silkscreen on canvas
72 × 80 in.

Agony Torn
2006
acrylic and silkscreen on canvas
44 × 34 in.

[from left to right]

Glass Doors
2006
felt marker on paper
11 × 17 in.

Untitled
2000
illustration
digital media direct to print

GEOFF MCFETRIDGE

Born: Edmonton, Alberta, Canada
Lives: Los Angeles, CA

When was the first time you exhibited your art in public?
My first real show was X-Large's gallery in LA.

It was a big opportunity and the right type of challenge at the right time for me.

Do you feel more comfortable in what you do now?
Very much so. I think I am still working as hard as I was back then, but with more efficiency and more joy. I think, when the challenges come, handling them stops being an issue.

What is the nicest compliment you've received about your work?
I have a photo of Arthur C. Clarke holding up a portrait I made of him. In the picture, he is smiling. I take that as a compliment.

How useful do you think a magazine like *Tokion* can be for an artist?
Magazines were a central way for me to show

my work when I started. Through the response to my work that was published, I got more work and made contacts that made it possible to support myself.

As far as you know, how have most people discovered your work, or what has gotten you the most attention?
T-shirts…

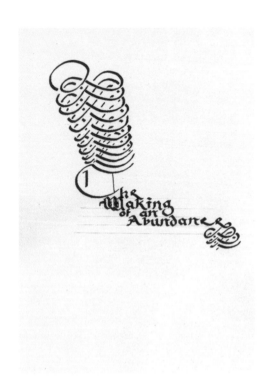

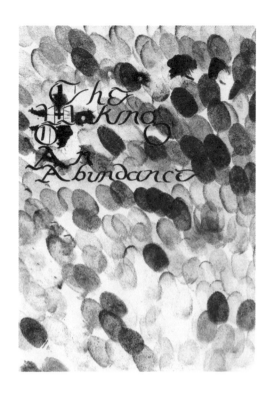

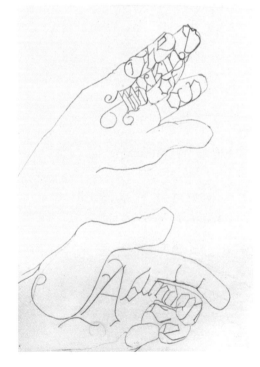

JESSE ALEXANDER

Born: Atlanta, Georgia
Lives: New York, NY

What was the first time you first exhibited your art in public?
In college, I made a flyer for a party. It was called the underwear party, so I drew some whitey-tighties and used the outline and seams as a map to get to the party.

What is the nicest compliment you've received for your work?
"I love you"—my wife.

What is the most frustrating thing to hear about your work?
As I'm essentially a commercial artist, the most frustrating thing is when people don't pay me when they promise to pay me. It makes me wonder about the value of my work, its place in society, and whether or not I can pay rent.

[clockwise from top left]

The Making of an Abundance (series)
2003
ink on paper
8 × 10 in.

JIMMY TURRELL

Born: Newcastle Upon Tyne, England
Lives: London, England

When was the first time you exhibited your art in public?
What was that experience like?
The National Centre for Popular Music, Sheffield,
in the UK in 1999. It was the first time I actually
saw large groups of people reacting to my work,
so it was all pretty nerve wracking. I tried to
stand near people when they were talking about
my work and try to listen in to their comments. I
know it's a bit sneaky, but I needed feedback.

What is one lesson you've learned since that time?
To be rigorous in my research. I'm obsessed
with finding the little eccentricities in life that
surround us everyday. A lot of my work is
steeped in nostalgia, but I try my hardest to
examine it in a contemporary setting. As an artist
I try to use methods that produce strange and
portentous combinations of images and ideas.
I want people to question my work.

How would you say your relationship to your work has
evolved since that time?
I guess I'm more analytical than I use to be. I
try to question my work and really examine the
roots of an idea and the effects that my work
may have.

If you could change one thing about how you make and
exhibit work, what would it be?
To make it move! Animation is the next step,
I think.

How useful do you think a magazine like *Tokion* can be for
an artist?
Speaking personally, working for *Tokion* was
incredibly useful for me. I got to work with
companies like Capitol Records, Nike, and
Colette Paris through the exposure from the
magazine.

The End
2006
illustration for a book by Chris Ashworth of
Getty Images
screen printed collage
46cm x 34cm

JON SANTOS

Born: Detroit, MI
Lives: New York City

When was the first time you exhibited your art in public?
I was designing rave flyers in Detroit back in the early '90s.

What was that experience like?
It wasn't considered a formal exhibition, so there was no horrifying pretense.

What is one lesson you've learned since that time?
The more you think about or analyze your "career," the worse off you are.

What is the nicest compliment you've received about your work?
I recently published a small book and the mother of a high school student ordered one for her son, and she was so excited about it. She said that he really loved it, and it was really important for her son's development.

What is the most frustrating thing to hear about your work?
That someone does not understand something that I thought was so obvious.

If you could change one thing about how you make and exhibit work, what would it be?
One thing I've thought a lot about recently is how to involve more performance in my work somehow. I'm not talking about "live painting." But maybe choreography, somehow.

[from left to right]

Time Traveller
2006
mixed media
5 × 5 in.

D
2006
mixed media
10 × 10 in.

JOSÉ PARLÁ

Born: Miami, FL
Lives: New York City

When was the first time you exhibited your art in public?
I've been making art in public since 1983, but my first exhibit in a museum was in 1988 at the Center for Fine Arts, in downtown Miami, Florida. I got a space in the show for receiving a Scholastic Art Award.

What was that experience like?
The experience was rewarding and frustrating. Frustrating because someone stole my artwork from the museum.

What is one lesson you've learned since that time?
Insure all artwork.

What is the most frustrating thing to hear about your work? Sometimes the public has a misinterpretation of a sub-culture and readily accepts what the media tells them. I meet people all the time from younger generations who do not care about history. That, to me, is a little disheartening.

As far as you know, how have most people discovered your work, or what has gotten you the most attention?
It is all connected, really. You have an exhibition, and if it's a good one people will tell their friends, and maybe a magazine covers it. Blogs nowadays can have a field day. The shows that exposed my work the most were the ones for which I got to paint really large-scale paintings.

[from left to right]

Brothers Back 2 Back
2006
collage, black gesso and posca paint
on canvas
6 × 6 in.

Ease in Deep Red
2006
mixed media, watercolor and dry pigment
on paper
30 × 44 in.

JOSH PETHERICK

Born: Adelaide, Australia
Lives: Melbourne, Australia

When was the first time you exhibited your art in public?
I started really young, doing hardcore fanzines and things like that. We'd write about records we were listening to, our friends' bands, semi-mythological rivalries with other facets of the punk community (namely the Christian and Nationalist hardcore bands going around at the time). I'd do all the graphics and montages and cartoons, too. We'd send these everywhere and didn't think twice about it.

What is one lesson you've learned since that time?
It's good to work around plant life. It makes a great deal of difference.

What is the nicest compliment you've received about your work?
"It looks like a child made it."

What is the most frustrating thing to hear about your work?
"It looks like a child made it."

If you could change one thing about how you make and exhibit work, what would it be?
Eradicate tendencies to procrastinate.

[from left to right]

Sewolawen
2007
mixed media on paper
39 × 61 in.

Mexico Drawing Series
2005
pencil and marker on paper
14 × 19 in. each

JULIE VERHOEVEN

Born: Sevenoaks, England
Lives: London, England

When was the first time you exhibited your art in public?
"Fat-Bottomed Girls" at Mobile Home in London,
in 2002. It was naïvely fun.

What is one lesson you've learned since that time?
I need to wash my hands and brushes
more regularly.

What is the nicest compliment you've received about
your work?
It gave someone a hard-on.

[from left to right]

Sweet Shuttlecock
acrylic and pen on paper
2006
12 × 16.5 in.

Button Bap
2006
acrylic and pen on paper
12 × 16.5 in.

Sun Rising
2002
pen and ink on paper
12 × 16.5 in.

KIM HIORTHØY

Born: Trondheim, Norway
Lives: Berlin, Germany

When was the first time you exhibited your art in public?
I had a sculpture in a kind of Christmas show at the local art museum in Trondheim when I was eighteen. It was an open show. Anyone could send work in.

What was that experience like?
I immediately thought I'd made it and that my path lay golden and shiny before me. When I realized that this was not true I felt very embarrassed.

What is one lesson you've learned since that time?
Don't listen to what people say about your work. Not when they say it's good and not when they say it's bad.

If you could change one thing about how you make and exhibit work, what would it be?
That I would truly not care what anybody said.

[from left to right]

Models
2007
drawing
16.5 × 11.5 in.

Untitled
2007
drawing
16.5 × 11.5 in.

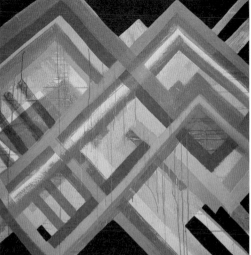

[from left to right]

*Everything Is Totally Going To Happen,
Vol. 1–13 (samples)*
2007
latex on canvas
48 × 48 in. and 24 × 24 in.

In You
2005
gouache and ink on baltic birch
12 × 19 in.

Magic Hands
2005
ink on vellum
16 × 20 in.

MAYA HAYUK

Born: Baltimore, MD
Lives: New York City

When was the first time you exhibited your art in public?
I never really had the nerve to share my paintings with people. In 1998 a roommate of mine in San Francisco suggested I curate a show, so I pulled together my favorite artists, found a gallery and went for it.

What was that experience like?
It was incredibly awesome, are you kidding? We painted all over the walls together, then everyone segued their work from one to the next, creating this fantastical, vibrant, tripped-out environment. The artists made a series of smaller work that we traded with each other and we all contributed to the music for the opening. It was one of the best things I've ever been a part of.

Do you feel more comfortable in what you do now?
Yes, so much. There's a flow from finding a safe place to take risks and in revisiting things I've let gestate for long periods of time. Alicia McCarthy had this painting that said "Hold On Let Go," and this mantra rings in my ears pretty loudly.

What is the nicest compliment you've received about your work?
Not getting painted over.

What is the most frustrating thing to hear about your work?
One time I was hanging my work in San Diego, years and years ago, and someone asked me whose work I was installing. He was like, "I thought it was a dude's."

How do you discover most artists you like?
On record covers and music show posters, through friends, in books, magazines, websites, galleries, museums (in that order).

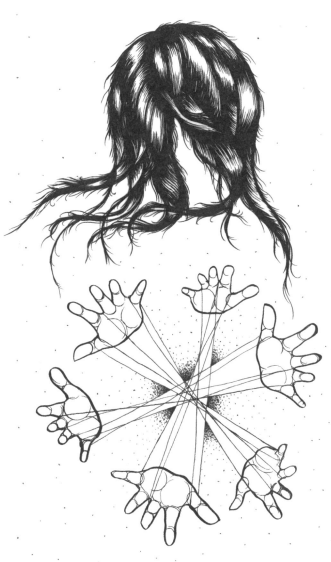

MIKE MILLS

Born: Berkeley, CA
Lives: Los Angeles, CA

When was the first time you exhibited your art in public?
Flyers I put up for my band in high school really feels like the first time. My first gallery show was at Alleged in, I don't know, '96 or '97.

What was that experience like?
Pretty great, especially because you have nothing to compare it to. Naïvete is so great, and you don't know you have it till it's gone. But I also remember one of my most trippy experiences was seeing posters I did for bands and [the clothing store] X-girl wheat-pasted in New York streets at the same time. For me, that's sort of the highest compliment: to be involved in the public sphere; to not be segregated into the art world.

What is one lesson you've learned since that time?
Why not just be yourself? No one else is doing that.

How would you say your relationship to your work has evolved since that time?
It's sort of my main way of experiencing and dealing with the world. That and the people I know. But like a lot of reformed shy people (which I am), making things can be a place where you feel more free, more able to try to figure out who you are. Not that that's really possible.

What is the nicest compliment you've received about your work?
There was this lady in the audience at Sundance. She was somehow afflicted with something—I couldn't tell what. Someone else asked me what my film was about, and the lady yelled out in frustration, "*Love.* It's about love."

What is the most frustrating thing to hear about your work?
It's "sweet."

How useful do you think a magazine like *Tokion* can be for an artist?
I think magazines are a great way to have an audience because they are public, relatively cheap, and a part of what we call "entertainment." But magazines can also be like heroin for our self-hatred—we are never like "them," those people in the magazines, even when we're in them. I have to look at them very, very sparingly, or else I don't feel good about myself anymore.

Humans 03 (Animal Rights)
2006
digital media
20 × 30 in.

WHAT HAPPENED?

NAGI NODA

Born: Tokyo, Japan
Lives: Tokyo, Japan

When was the first time you exhibited your art in public?
I did an exhibition of big drawings when I was twenty-three.

What was that experience like?
I painted whatever came to my mind at that time, so it was really natural for me to present my work.

What is one lesson you've learned since that time?
Since the exhibition, I have started to execute my ideas and my world as much as I can. Creation, for me, is about expressing my pains, the meaning of life—all the different feelings one may have, such as happiness, love, etc. Creating works is extremely important for me because it is a process of confronting my feelings and summarizing them.

How would you say your relationship to your work has evolved since that time?
I grew up in an artistic environment; both of my parents were artists. So it has always been very natural for me to do what I do.

How do you discover most artists you like?
It all depends, but usually I become friends with them first before I fall in love with their work. It is difficult to like someone's work in a deeper sense without knowing the connection between their personality and their work.

[from left to right]

Untitled
print
digital media

Untitled
2004
print
digital media

NOAH BUTKUS

Born: Hartford, CT
Lives: New York City

When was the first time you exhibited your art in public?
I used to draw flyers for my brother's and his friends' hardcore bands in Connecticut. That was the first sort of art I made that anyone who didn't know me personally could have seen.

What was that experience like?
It was a lot fun. My brother was into anything I drew for him.

What is one lesson you've learned since that time?
When I was younger, I would spend days on one drawing, really taking my time with it. Now I can't seem to spend more that a few hours on a drawing. My focus is really up and down.

How would you say your relationship to your work has evolved since that time?
I feel more connected to my drawing now. I don't feel like I was drawing from within my self when I was younger. I would push my drawings really hard to get to where I wanted them, and that's why I would spend so much time on them.

What is the nicest compliment you've received about your work?
I guess when people ask me if they can get tattoos of my drawings. That's cool—to hear that someone likes your stuff that much, to permanently put it on their bodies.

If you could change one thing about how you make and exhibit work, what would it be?
Exhibits are tough for me, mentally. I've never really been too outward about my work. Everything I draw or make is for my own consumption. To have people coming to a gallery to look at my stuff adds a lot of weight to it, because at the that point I feel I have a duty to make something that's interesting for other people to look at. But I really need to just be focused on what I like and trust my gut.

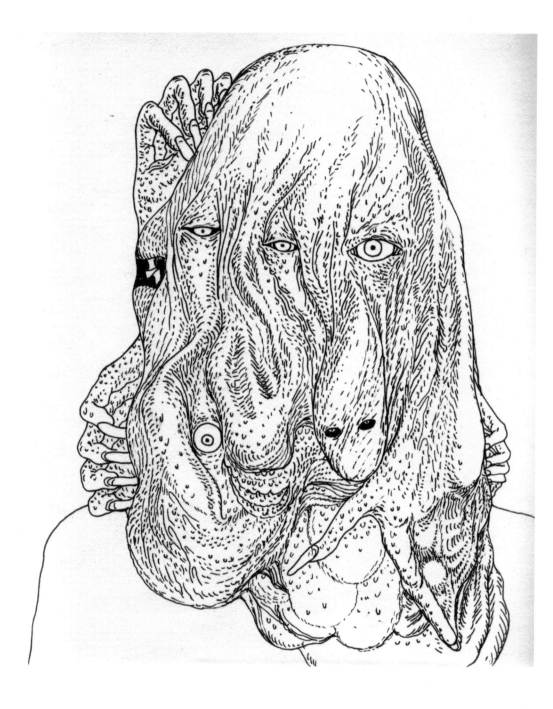

MELT YER FACE
2006
black pen on basic drawing paper

Untitled
2006
ballpoint pen on construction paper

PERKS & MINI

a.k.a. Misha Hollenbach, Dennis Roussos, and Roland Korg
Born: Burwood, Melbourne, Australia
Live: in our heads

When was the first time you exhibited your art in public?
I put some work in a free exhibition that was part of an aboriginal festival in Melbourne when I was fourteen.

What was that experience like? .
For me, the payoff is the work itself. If people see it, great. If not, that's great, too. So the experience of showing, to me, isn't all that exciting.

What is the nicest compliment you've received about your work?
I like it when kids enjoy the work. They're untainted. And natural.

What is the most frustrating thing to hear about your work?
Questions.

If you could change one thing about how you make and exhibit work, what would it be?
I have a dream to live in seclusion with my wife and make work, but to also make tofu and love.

Aliens & Dolphins
2005
acrylic, silkscreen and spray paint on paper,
edition of seven
30 × 42 in.

Moz Art
2007
C-print
110 cm × 187 cm

ROSTARR

Born: Daegu, South Korea
Lives: New York City

When was the first time you exhibited your art in public?
The first time I exhibited my art in public was straight out of college in a show called "Romon Exposition" at KRT, a fashion PR firm in the Meatpacking district in New York around 1994.

What was that experience like?
I was pretty nervous, because my friends at the time were all blowing up in the art and fashion worlds, and I didn't really consider my work to be up to par yet.

What is one lesson you've learned since that time?
I learned that no one wants you to be an artist, especially other artists.

What is the nicest compliment you've received about your work?
I like it when reviews say, "If you like so and so's work, then you'll love Rostarr."

What is the most frustrating thing to hear about your work?
To be considered an underground or street artist.

If you could change one thing about how you make and exhibit work, what would it be?
I wouldn't change a thing. It's the minds in the art world that need changing.

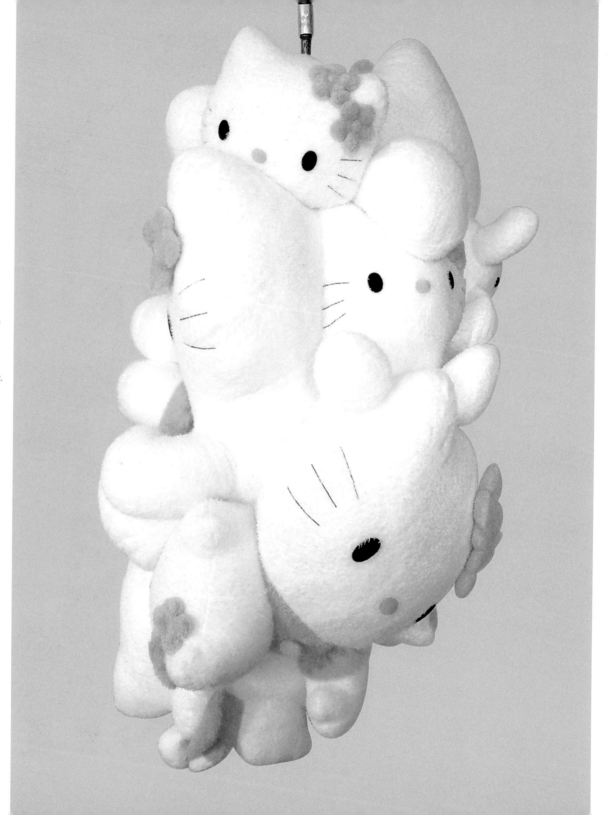

[from left to right]

Polymorphic Kittyclysm
2005
polyester fiber, thread and bike chain
45 × 28 in. diameter

Siamese Antichrist
2006
Sumi ink on handmade paper
52 × 36 in.

RYAN MCGINNESS

Born: Virginia Beach, VA
Lives: New York City

What is the nicest compliment you've received about your work?
The simplest compliment, "I like your work," is the nicest.

What is the most frustrating thing to hear about your work?
People often think that I use logos, but I actually assume the visual language of corporate identities and create drawings that subvert the anonymous power of those forms.

If you could change one thing about how you make and exhibit work, what would it be?
I am constantly trying to improve and develop my systems of production, which include researching different pigments and experimenting with different formats.

[from left to right]

Latet Anguis In Herba
2006
acrylic on wood panel
48 × 48 in.

Sol Lucet Omnibus
2006
acrylic on linen
96 × 96 in.

[from left to right]

Yao Ming
2004
digital
8.5 × 10.25 in.

Gubbish
2007
acrylic and digital
8.5 × 11 in.

SAIMAN CHOW

Born: Hong Kong
Lives: New York City

When was the first time you exhibited your art in public?
When I was living in a loft complex in downtown Los Angeles, every year there was an art walk event in which artists in every studio exhibited their works to public.

What was that experience like?
It was pretty exciting and rewarding, actually, I sold my first painting for $500. It was a pretty big deal for me at that time. I sold it to this guy name Danny First, whose claim to fame was doodling these childlike stick figures printed on T-shirts and other products. They were huge back in the '80s and were sold everywhere. My brother and I went to his giant mansion in Hollywood to deliver the painting. His house was unbelievably huge, and he had eight rooms just to hang artwork.

How would you say your relationship to your work has evolved since that time?
My work changes every day. I just try to go with whatever I have in my head and just do what I feel like at the moment. I admire people who can maintain consistency and develop a unique language. I'm just not capable of doing so.

What is the nicest compliment you've received about your work?
"What kind of drugs you take?"

What is the most frustrating thing to hear about your work?
"I like your older work better."

As far as you know, how have most people discovered your work, or what has gotten you the most attention?
The turning point of my career was after I did an animation for Nike called "Art of Speed." That piece got lots of attention and press. I was also hated by many people after that.

SHEPARD FAIREY

Born: Charleston, SC
Lives: Los Angeles, CA

When was the first time you exhibited your art in public?
When I was fifteen I started making a lot of my own versions of punk rock bands' logos. Making T-shirts and cutting stencils and spray-painting them onto three-packs of T-shirts I'd buy at Wal-Mart. I guess the first thing I did that was, even tough it was kind of derivative of pop culture, was when I started doing the Andre the Giant stickers when I was nineteen. In a lot of ways, I was too chicken to ask for a café art show, and that gave me the confidence.

What is one lesson you've learned since that time?
You have to persevere and trust your own judgment. Whether it's your teachers in art school or people who run a gallery who want to tell you what will sell, there is a peanut gallery that wants to tell you how to live your life and what you should be doing. In the end, it's you who has to live your life and be happy with what you're doing. Every time I've second-guessed myself, it's been a mistake.

How would you say your relationship to your work has evolved since that time?
What people respond to in art is that it is that artist's idiosyncratic vision. That's what makes it art, as compared to other visual communication that's going for the lowest common denominator.

[from left to right]

Vivienne Westwood
2005
mixed media on collage paper
30 × 43 in.

Guns and Roses
2006
mixed media on collage paper
30 × 43 in.

As I've gained confidence, my visual language has evolved and diversified. It's much more singular, in that it doesn't have such an obvious connection to an existing genre.

I've had several people tell me they were going to go to liberal arts college but decided to become designers because of my work. That I've actually changed their lives is insane. It's not because of how awesome I am. It's because of how mediocre I am. I show that if you stick to it, you can succeed.

That my work is just recycled Soviet constructivist propaganda stuff, and I'm a sellout and that my politics are just a hollow pose.

Obviously, on the street, though now there's a lot on the Internet. I try to put myself out there in many, many ways. I never look down on commercial work, because I discovered a lot of my favorite artists, such as Mike Mills or Raymond Pettibon, that way. It's like a trickle *up* effect.

RELAX RELAX RELAX RELAX RELAX
RELAX RELAX RELAX RELAX REL
RELAX RELAX RELAX RELAX REL
RELAX! RELAX! RELAX RELAX R EL
RELAX RELAX! RELAX RELAX
RELAX!

SUN AN

Born: Seoul, South Korea
Lives: Los Angeles, CA

When was the first time you exhibited your art in public?
I guess the first time was on the Internet in the late '90s. It was a weird time. I was about eighteen.

What was that experience like?
I had no idea about what would happen, and didn't expect anything from it. Then I was nervous when people looked and responded. I felt like I had been found and I had no idea what I was doing, really. At that time, the community of all these web sites and artists/designers was small, so it was easy to recognize new sites. It was all there, always being updated. It was really an amazing thing, and being really young while these changes were taking place was kind of amazing. Everyone had similar tools, so you could not tell if these sites were real studios or just another kid making stuff.

How would you say your relationship to your work has evolved since that time?
I am still trying to figure out how my work and my life connect. There's an ideal way to go about things, but it's always a game of mix and match, so I try my best to maintain balance and have a clear state of mind.

What is the most frustrating thing to hear about your work?
I appreciate any and all criticism.

If you could change one thing about how you make and exhibit work, what would it be?
I would like to eliminate the idea of self-promotion. I'm just not very good at that.

[from left to right]

Relax Dude
2006
T-shirt

Why Are Designers So Concerned With the Professionalization of their Activity?
2006
Animation / Video
720 × 480 pixels

SWOON

Born: New London, CT
Lives: New York City

When was the first time you exhibited your art in public?
I was sixteen and there was one little punk club/café/alternative art venue in my town. Getting up the gumption to ask them to show my stuff was harrowing, and when they did, I felt like such a super star.

What was that experience like?
It was really strange that suddenly people who knew me only from dancing at the punk show now suddenly had this window into my inner life. I went from being the quiet girl to a more multi-dimensional person in the eyes of my peers, and I could tell the difference immediately. I think it created a kind of a positive feedback loop, and it did wonders.

What is one lesson you've learned since that time?
Find your community, stand by them, work with people you love, and don't bother with people that skeeve you out. Also, don't wait for your context, create one for yourself. Sometimes the world is not going to know it's ready for you till you get there.

How would you say your relationship to your work has evolved since that time?
I am a lot less "realistic" in my expectations of myself now than I was then. When I was real small, I loved horses. Then my big dream was wanting to be a jockey. But instead I dreamed of being a stable hand, because I didn't want to ask too much of myself and the world. Somewhere along the line, there came a blossoming. Now, if something doesn't make me jittery with nervousness, I have a hard time focusing.

What is the nicest compliment you've received about your work?
A woman in Portland, Oregon, told me that my work made her feel less alone in the world. What could be better than that?

What is the most frustrating thing to hear about your work?
Some people believe that my work's eventual inclusion in institutional contexts somehow erases the importance of the direct experience that people have with my portraits on the street. I find the people who go out and vandalize my work on these grounds to be hugely frustrating and arrogant. They are thinking only of their petty intellectual qualms and not about the human experience of what is made—thinking about theory and hard-line political stances and not about the guy who lives on the block, who at

the end of the day, the work is for. That kind of stupidity gets me heated.

If you could change one thing about how you make and exhibit work, what would it be?
I am trying to figure out more and more ways that my work can weave itself into daily contexts. The ways in which we are supposed to experience art

are boring and unimaginative. I come from a small town, and I know that most people feel the same way: When they see so much of modern art, they think that the joke must be on them. I know that I am not going to be able to communicate with everyone, but I am willing to give an honest shot at making an honest thing.

[from left to right]

Untitled
2007
Wheat paste on wall
Pinchuk Art Center, Ukraine

Untitled
2007
Wheat paste on wall
Pinchuk Art Center, Ukraine

ANDREW ASHLEY MACOMBER
JEFFREY WRIGHT KEVIN LYONS
Margaret KILGALLEN
BARRY McGEE J PENRY
Eddie MARTINEZ
BRENDAN gordon HULL
DONNELLY
JIM HOUSER
CLARE ROJAS CHRIS
DAVID SHRIGLEY JOHANSON

KEEGAN McHARGUE

Misaki KAWAI

Simone SHUBUCK

ED TEMPLETON JO JACKSON

THOMAS CAMPBELL

RICH JACOBS Matt LEINES

MARCEL DZAMA OS GEMEOS

TIFFANY MALAKOOTI

TOMOO GOKITA WeS LANG

a swatch of houndstooth fabric drinking with a drawing

[from left to right]

A Swatch of Houndstooth
2006
paint, pencil and collage on paper
8 × 10 in.

Weekend Drugs
2006
acrylic on panel
16 × 20 in.

Graffiti School
2006
oil on panel
21.5 × 16.5 in.

ANDREW JEFFREY WRIGHT

Born: St. Petersburg, FL
Lives: Philadelphia, PA

When was the first time you exhibited your art in public?
Around 1980, at an art show at the Springfield Mall in suburban Philadelphia.

What was that experience like?
One of my best friends won an award at that show. I thought my drawing was just as good and was confused as to why I didn't win an award. My mom pointed out that the theme of the show was "my neighborhood," and my drawing was a self-portrait of me kicking a hacky sack in front of a dilapidated, graffiti-covered fence. She explained people don't want to see a graffiti-covered fence—they want to see something nice about the neighborhood. My drawing was a bit of a farce, anyway, because in real life I didn't kick a hacky sack in front of graffiti-covered fence. I just thought that was a more interesting background than some bushes.

What is one lesson you've learned since that time?
Everybody is an artist and everything is art.

How would you say your relationship to your work has evolved since that time?
It hasn't really evolved and I feel great!

Weekend drugs

next week in graffiti School

— running from the cops
— hiding it in your coat
— achieving fame for blocks (at least 3 blocks)
— one handed double does
— stabbing and face slicing
— narcing on your friends and moving to another City

ASHLEY MACOMBER

Born: Hartford, CT
Lives: Los Angeles, CA

When was the first time you exhibited your art in public?
When I was a junior in high school I entered a statewide competition and won some sort of prize. There was a show in Boston with like 200 pieces of art in this convention center.

What was that experience like?
It was overwhelming to realize how much art is made on a daily basis, by people my own age. It made my competitive nature come alive.

What is one lesson you've learned since that time?
Label your art correctly so it doesn't get hung upside down.

How would you say your relationship to your work has evolved since that time?
I am learning what kinds of expectations to have with my work. I've learned that showing it to the world is an epic gift but you shouldn't give it the power to make you feel good. It is too transient and temporal for that.

What is the nicest compliment you've received about your work?
Someone once said that they were glad that I was born into the world. Compliments like that are tricky, though, because it is placing a person's worth on what they produce.

If you could change one thing about how you make and exhibit work, what would it be?
I would have a house in the woods where I could go for a month or two at a time to have some mental space. In other words, I would have the money to take my time.

|from left to right|

Schematic Gesture #1
2006
acrylic and gouache on paper
22 × 28 in.

Petrouchka
2006
acrylic and gouache on paper
30 × 46 in.

BARRY MCGEE

Born: San Francisco, CA
Lives: San Francisco, CA

When was the first time you exhibited your art in public?
What was that experience like?
I think it was in 1985, and it was a terrible
mistake that I'm still paying for.

What is one lesson you've learned since that time?
Becoming invisible.

What is the nicest compliment you've received about
your work?
"You are under arrest."

If you could change one thing about how you make and
exhibit work, what would it be?
My name.

[from left to right]

Untitled

Untitled

Untitled

Untitled

BRENDAN DONNELLY

Born: Connecticut
Lives: New York City

When was the first time you exhibited your art in public?
The most *recent* public art project I've done so far is illustrations for the windows of the MTV store in Times Square. It wraps around the block. I've done art shows, murals, T-shirts, cartoons, and illustrations, but this is the work I'm most proud of.

Do you have a peer network that supports you in your work?
My friends are the biggest support and pain in the ass. They get on my case for not working enough and upset if I'm not hanging out enough. I can never win. I would take a bullet for them.

Well, maybe not a bullet but a riot-control beanbag bullet.

How useful do you think a magazine like *Tokion* can be for an artist?
Tokion gave me my first opportunity to show my work and gave me more opportunities over the years. From there on, I was able to understand how to be confident about showing work and ideas, how to get press and network with other artists and magazines. I met a lot of really cool people that I'm friends with to this day. So yes, magazines are very helpful, if you find the right one.

[from left to right]

Ghost Ships
2005
ink, pencil, watercolor, and acrylic on paper
24 × 36 in.

Joy Division in Arabic
2004
screen print on vintage shirt

Untitled
2005
ink on paper
14 × 17 in.

Ramones in Arabic
2004
screen print on vintage shirt

Untitled (Abstract)
2006
acrylic on wood
78 × 72 in.

Untitled (Connected Souls…)
2006
acrylic on paper
26 × 38 in.

CHRIS JOHANSON

Born: San Jose, CA
Lives: Portland, OR

When was the first time you exhibited your art in public?
The first time in San Francisco was at Café Picarro, I think. I am not totally sure because I showed at a lot of cafés before having a show in a commercial gallery.

What was that experience like?
It was a good experience. I like cafés alot. And I really liked being young and in outer space and showing my pictures in cafés in San Francisco with all these bohemian types of people. Picarro had lots of local mellow music, like this guy named Omar who a lot of people in the Mission District called "the troll." He played guitar and his girlfriend played tambourine. That was my favorite café.

What is one lesson you've learned since that time?
One lesson I've learned is that when you are twenty you can quite possibly know a lot less than you can when you are thirty-eight. That is at least the case with me.

CLARE ROJAS

Born: Columbus, OH
Lives: San Francisco, CA

When was the first time you exhibited your art in public?
The first show I had was in my town's public library.

How would you say your relationship to your work has evolved since that time?
Let's just say nowadays, I live to work, instead of work to live.

What is the nicest compliment you've received about your work?
When the moms and the kids and the cleaning ladies can walk into my show and laugh and give each other high fives, it really makes my day.

[from left to right]

Bird Throated
2005
gouache and latex on panel
11 × 7 in.

Lonely Judged on Turquoise
2005
gouache and latex on panel
10 × 12 in.

DAVID SHRIGLEY

Born: MacClesfield, England
Lives: Glasgow, Scotland.

When was the first time you exhibited your art in public?
The first work that I had exhibited was at school when I was fourteen. I painted a picture of me shooting the queen. They removed it from the exhibition, and I had to go and see the principal of the school and explain myself.

What is one lesson you've learned since that time?
I should have more respect for the monarchy.

How would you say your relationship to your work has evolved since that time?
I think I am a better artist now than I was at fourteen.

What is the nicest compliment you've received about your work?
To be honest I only remember the bad things people say.

[from left to right]

Untitled
2006
ink on paper
20 × 9 in.

Untitled
1995
ink on paper
11.5 × 16.5 in.

ARTISTS

 TALK ABOUT THEIR WORK

I DON'T ACTUALLY DO THE PAINTINGS MYSELF, I GET A BUNCH OF HANDICAPPED KIDS TO DO THEM FOR ME....

I USE A LOT OF FOUND MATERIALS IN MY WORK. MY LATEST PIECE IS FIFTY IDENTICAL PAIRS OF CHILDRENS SHOES WHICH I FOUND IN A CHARITY SHOP THEY'RE BRILLIANT AND THEY ONLY COST £30.

I WENT AROUND TOWN AND ASKED DOSSERS IF I COULD BUY THEIR UNDERPANTS FROM THEM. I GOT SIX PAIRS FOR £5 EACH AND USED THEM FOR MY SHOW IN FRANCE.

I GO AROUND BARS AT THE WEEKENDS AND DELIBERATELY GET INTO FIGHTS AND GET MY HEAD KICKED IN WHILE A FRIEND OF MINE VIDEOS IT.

THE JUDAS GOAT LEADS THE OTHERS INTO THE SLAUGHTERHOUSE

these are the red-eye politics

ED TEMPLETON

Born: Orange County, CA
Lives: Huntington Beach, CA

When was the first time you exhibited your art in public?
I think it was in 1992 or '93 in LA. It was a two-day show in an abandoned building called "48 Hours in the Hole." But as far as a fully formed non-cattle-call type of thing, it was in 1993, at a skateboarder art show called "The Degenerates" curated by Dan Field at some gallery in Chicago. I remember having dinner with Mark Gonzalez and Matt Hensley, and some real scary skinhead guy came to our table to fuck with us, and Mark got up and yelled at him. I thought, "We are all dead," but nothing happened.

What was that experience like?
It was real exciting, truthfully. To have another person or bunch of people consider what you painted is very fun. It's the opening of a conversation.

What is one lesson you've learned since that time?
I learned that most galleries look like hospitals, and perhaps they shouldn't . . .

Do you feel more comfortable in what you do now?
For sure, but the more comfortable you get, the harder it is to change.

Who do you consider to be your peers?
All of humanity. I'm not trying to be cute when I say that. I thought about that question. My line of thinking went from naming a bunch of people, which I thought would be weird, to just "all artists." But then, why would I limit it? All living creatures are sharing this experience on earth at this time. I know that sounds like some hippie shit, but whatever.

What is the nicest compliment you've received about your work?
Someone said it "reads like a good book," which I thought was very nice.

As far as you know, how have most people discovered your work, or what has gotten you the most attention?
I think I have benefited greatly from the skateboard world, which is very supportive; and it helps make the art world less stuffy. The openings are peppered with sweaty skateboard-carrying kids, helping dilute the dressed-up art hipsters a bit.

EDDIE MARTINEZ

Born: Groton, CT
Lives: New York City

When was the first time you exhibited your art in public?
In 1996 I had my first group show in Boston.

What is one lesson you've learned since that time?
You shouldn't be afraid of self-promotion. It seems like a lot of artists think that it's lame, but it helps you a lot.

What is the nicest compliment you've received about your work?
People have told me that my art has an effortless look to it.

What is the most frustrating thing to hear about your work?
"Is that archival?"

If you could change one thing about how you make and exhibit work, what would it be?
I think what is most important is to keep pushing my work and see where it goes, rather than worrying about what to do differently.

[from left to right]

Polkadot Playa
2005
enamel and acrylic on paper
16 × 11 in.

The Great Stare Down
2005
acrylic on wood
48 × 60 in.

GORDON HULL

Born: New York City
Lives: New York City

When was the first time you exhibited your art in public?
Toward the end of my freshman year at NYU, I started tracing shadows in chalk around downtown Manhattan—objects, people, whatever. Tagging shadows . . .

What was that experience like?
At the time, I thought it was really exciting. I was new to the city and was just kind of exploring and having fun. I didn't know shit about graffiti or street art or anything like that. I just thought it was cool that lots of people would see my work the next day.

What is one lesson you've learned since that time?
If you work in the street, don't get caught. Aside from that, I think the most important lesson I have ever learned about making art is to just keep on making it.

How would you say your relationship to your work has evolved since that time?
I think the process of being an artist is obviously one of continual growth. You can have confidence but no comfort. The uncomfortable space that an artist inhabits—that's the part that drives you to create something better every time.

What is the nicest compliment you've received about your work?
Some girl I have never met had a drawing of mine tattooed on herself.

What is the most frustrating thing to hear about your work?
"I don't get it."

AN ARRANGEMENT
OF FLOWERS

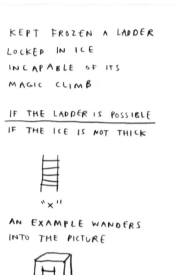

KEPT FROZEN A LADDER
LOCKED IN ICE
INCAPABLE OF ITS
MAGIC CLIMB

IF THE LADDER IS POSSIBLE
IF THE ICE IS NOT THICK

"X"

AN EXAMPLE WANDERS
INTO THE PICTURE

THIS IS A LADDER
FROZEN IN ICE

A SECRET WHISPERED
INTO A FIST AND
THROWN

"GUMSHOE"

[from left to right]

An Arrangement of Flowers
2006
graphite and ink on paper
18 × 24 in.

Frozen A Ladder
2005
graphite and ink on paper
20 × 24 in.

A Secret Whispered
2006
graphite and ink on paper
20 × 24 in.

A Ship In The Night
2006
graphite and ink on paper
20 × 24 in.

A SHIP IN THE NIGHT
WITH THE NIGHT
CUT OUT

J PENRY

Born: Daphne, AL
Lives: New York City

When was the first time you exhibited your art in public?
In college, I knew two rowdy dudes who had art shows in their apartment. They were skaters, so they liked immature drawings like the ones I did. They asked me to hang some stuff and then we got wasted and broke stuff with a ladder.

What was that experience like?
I was just happy to not be on the farm.

What is one lesson you've learned since that time?
That Picasso quote about unlearning how to make art to make better art doesn't really apply in the real world, unless you're a midget already famous for drawing badly.

How would you say your relationship to your work has evolved since that time?
I've just reverted back into my OCD high-school style of cross-hatching.

What is the nicest compliment you've received about your work?
I was told that Keith Morris from Black Flag and Walter from Youth of Today were into some stuff I did. I was flattered.

[from left to right]

Corrine
2006
ink on paper
8.5 × 11 in.

Perfect
2002
ink on paper
5 × 8 in.

Girls Are Easy To Draw
2003
ink on paper
6 × 11 in.

JIM HOUSER

Born: Philadelphia, PA
Lives: Philadelphia, PA

When was the first time you exhibited your art in public?
Probably the grand opening of the art gallery
Space 1026, in 1997. The first show was a
group show. I had my first solo show there
in 1998.

What was that experience like?
I have good memories of the early days of 1026.
We were all young and had no idea what we
were doing, but it all worked out. It made me
feel like I had finally found a job I would be able
to do.

What is one lesson you've learned since that time?
I've learned it's important to say no to things. I
used to do every show anyone asked me to be
in. It's a good way to burn yourself out. I guess I
learned the limit of how hard I can work.

**How would you say your relationship to your work has
evolved since that time?**
Well, painting has become what defines me as
a person. I have had some rough times, and
painting has always been there.

**What is the nicest compliment you've received about
your work?**
A fourteen-year-old kid once bought one of
my paintings at an opening, with money he had
been saving up to buy a video game. I can't
imagine the fourteen-year-old me doing that.

[from left to right]

We Know
2007
acrylic on wood
8 ×11 in.

FTW
2006
acrylic and collage on canvas 18 × 24 in.
(Both shot by Chris Searl)

[from left to right]

Glacier
2006
acrylic and gouache on paper
8 × 12.25 in.

Living Brushes
2006
ink and watercolor on paper
20 × 14 in.

Keys, No Lock
2006
ink and watercolor on paper
16 × 20.25 in.

JO JACKSON

Lives: Portland, OR

When was the first time you exhibited your art in public?
I made a mini-comic in Washington, DC. It was sold out of a little cardboard display box that I made that sat on the counter of some vintage stores and a book store.

What was that experience like?
I felt very embarrassed and kind of ashamed. DC seemed so strict—the laws of what was "cool" and what was "not cool" seemed really serious. I was pretty young! But it is a big deal to put your art into the public, like dreams of being on the bus with no pants on. It's still difficult, even now.

How would you say your relationship to your work has evolved since that time?
At that time, I was making art as an escape from my regular life. Now it *is* my regular life. It's harder now.

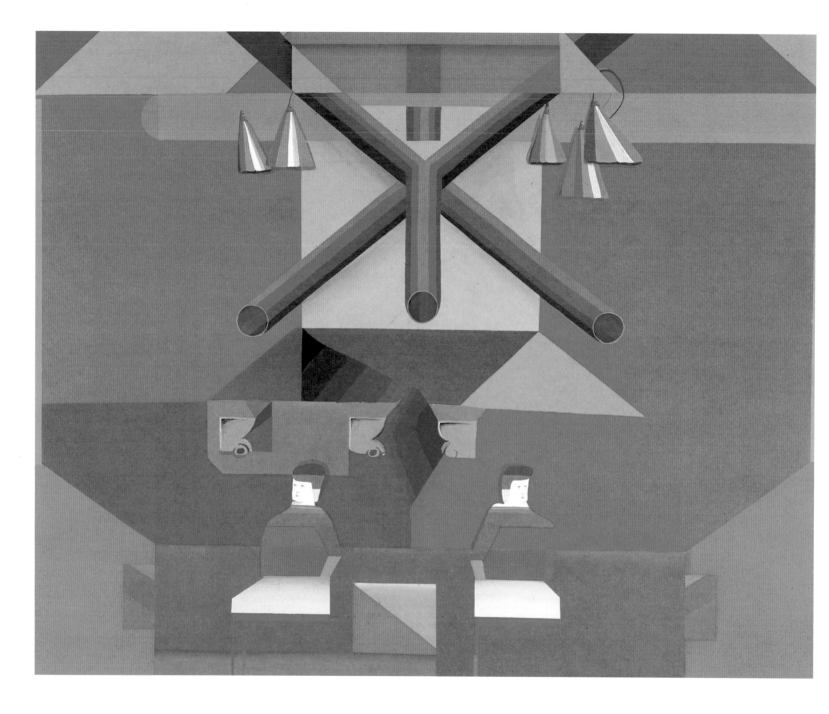

[from left to right]

Busts
2005
acrylic on panel
40 × 50 in.

Descent
2006
acrylic on panel
40 × 50 in.

KEEGAN MCHARGUE

Born: Portland, OR
Lives: San Francisco, California

When was the first time you exhibited your art in public?
I think it was in 2002, in LA. I was on an anti–Thomas Edison kick at the time and, ironically, there was a power outage on the block of the gallery that night. No one could even see the work.

What was that experience like?
It was dark, literally. I was very excited and happy, but I knew it was just a steppingstone. I was twenty.

What is one lesson you've learned since that time?
I have learned that less is actually more, just like they say.

How would you say your relationship to your work has evolved since that time?
I feel more like an idea person now, while then I felt more like an "artist" toiling away with my tools. Now, once the idea is set in stone, the pieces paint themselves. I put less emphasis on virtuosity.

What is the most frustrating thing to hear about your work?
The more people who know about it and have seen it, the more people there will be who dislike it. I have seen honest visceral reactions in people after coming from my shows. That's OK, and can be taken as a compliment in some way. The most frustrating thing is people being jealous of your success, as if there is only a certain amount of success available in the world, and I am taking a portion of what they feel should be theirs.

How useful do you think a magazine like *Tokion* can be for an artist?
Tokion is great. I love the mix of art and celebrity and pop. It's like what Andy Warhol wanted *Interview* to be. In Europe, many artists' names are commonplace, but I think you would be hard pressed to find many Americans able to name even the most successful of artists. The more information that gets out to the masses the better, in my opinion.

As far as you know, how have most people discovered your work, or what has gotten you the most attention?
I think I have, for better or worse, attracted media attention. I got rated in the top twenty-five "hottest" people under twenty-five by a largely distributed monthly (that I don't personally read), and I had all sorts of people calling me saying, "I saw you beat out Nicole Richie on the top twenty-five." Maybe someday I will actually get attention for my work, but for now I will enjoy that flash heat of the pop world.

95

MATT LEINES

Born: Totowa, NJ
Lives: Montclair, NJ

When was the first time you exhibited your art in public?
The first time I remember my work being
exhibited was in first grade, for the bicentennial
of my hometown, Totowa, New Jersey. I did a
drawing of a house across the street from our
school. It was one of the many "Washington
slept here" colonial houses in New Jersey.

What was that experience like?
I don't remember much about it, other than I
know my grandma saw it.

What is one lesson you've learned since that time?
The one thing I always go back to is something
my high school art teacher used to say. Something like, "You think on the page, not in
your head."

Do you feel more comfortable in what you do now?
Most problems I've had making things have
been with materials. Running out of a certain
ink and then not being able to find another
jar or finding out that something has been
discontinued can be really frustrating. But
other times the ideas seem to run out, and
it's a struggle to even sketch things out.

What is the nicest compliment you've received about
your work?
When I had just graduated from school, I found
out that Jo Jackson and Chris Johanson owned
a tiny painting I had made. I flipped out and
shared the news with anyone within earshot,
99 percent of whom had no idea who I was
talking about.

|from left to right|

Fortune Tree
2006
watercolor and ink on paper
11 × 8.5 in.

King of the Men in the Sky
2006
watercolor and ink on paper
16 × 12 in.

MISAKI KAWAI

Born: Osaka, Japan
Lives: New York City

When was the first time you exhibited your art in public?
When I was an art student, me and two of my best friends grabbed some artwork we made and a CD player, then we went to Sanjyo Kiya-machi in Kyoto. We found a little spot to hang out and put music on and danced a little bit and put some artwork that we brought out on the street. We called it "Guerilla Gallery."

What was that experience like?
It was mostly just a lot of fun. We were getting feedback from a lot of people who were walking by, and a lot of homeless people who were hanging around. One man bought three of my prints for about ten dollars. That was the first time I made money with my art.

How would you say your relationship to your work has evolved since that time?
I've learned a lot more about how to make a living as an artist. It's really hard to find out how to make a living as an artist. Many of my friends from art school have ended up working for design companies.

What is the nicest compliment you've received about your work?
It's so funny how American people are very open to show how they feel. So some people have big gestures to show me how much they like my work. That's very nice.

What is the most frustrating thing to hear about your work?
When people think I'm trying to just make cute pop art. I like cute images, but mostly ones that are so cute that it's stupid. I like more raw and bad-style things. I think a lot of people don't see the difference between that and a more serious kind of pop cute.

[from left to right]

Untitled Wave
2005
collage and gouache on paper
15.75 × 17.75 in.

Welcome Home
2005
collage and gouache on paper
15.75 × 24 in.

Pink Skate Ramp
2005
collage, ink and gouache on paper
15.75 × 24 in.

Wild Tiger Drip
2005
ink and gouache on paper
8.25 × 11 in.

KEVIN LYONS

Born: CT
Lives: Philadelphia, PA

When was the first time you exhibited your art in public?
Most would not coin me an artist, so my shit
has really been public since I started doing it.

What is one lesson you've learned since that time?
No matter how much you want it to, nothing
really ever works out the way you want it to. I
am not sure what that is all about, but every
show is never as good as you wanted it to be.
So you are continually pressing on in hopes of . . .
what? Ideally, you start out to get recognized.
Then it is about who you work for, and then it
becomes about money and creative control. It
is always something else. The body of work
and the enjoyment often get lost. I got in this
game to do something I enjoy doing rather than
working a normal job. Well, it is easy to stray
from that, and it gets easier as you buy into
it all. You have to stay true to what you set out
to do. And hope to make rent and eat a little
here and there.

**How would you say your relationship to your work has
evolved since that time?**
Well the most significant thing is now they want
me for me. I get to do what I want, and the
job and look is no longer dictated to me. I am
appreciated for simply doing what I do.

**What is the most frustrating thing to hear about
your work?**
That people don't know its mine.

**How useful do you think a magazine like *Tokion* can be for
an artist?**
I think a magazine can reinforce an artist's work
and obviously gain some PR for an artist. But
artists can do a ton for a magazine. The artists,
photographers, and writers who did work for
Tokion made *Tokion* what it is. The magazine
was not the star of the show. The artists who
were in it were the focus. You picked it up for
them, and that is what makes *Tokion* special.

[from left to right]

Yokohama
2006
marks-a-lot on paper
16 × 16 in.

Sketch Number 1
2006
marks-a-lot on paper
16 × 16 in.

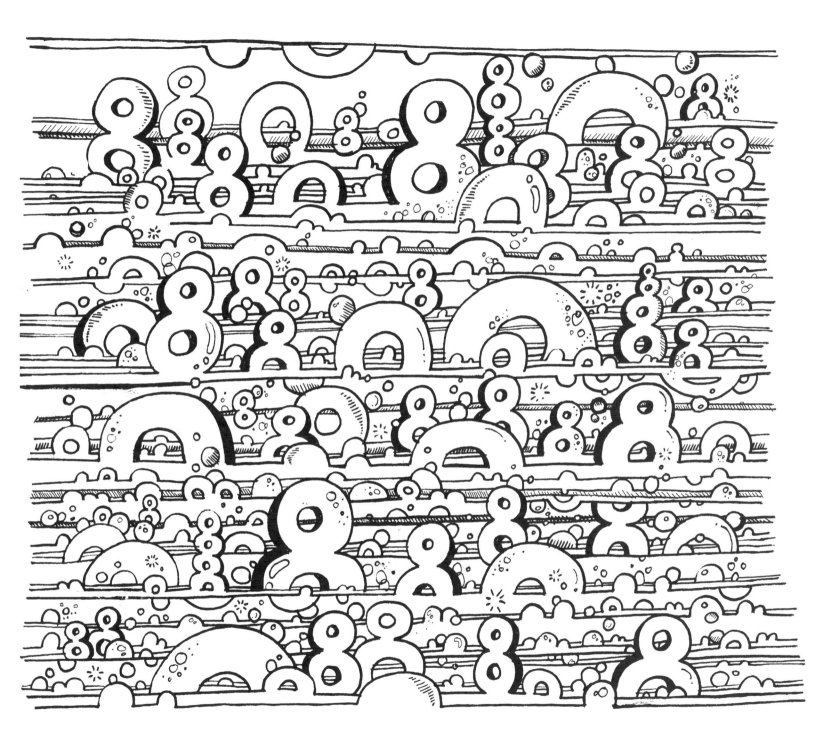

MARCEL DZAMA

Born: Winnipeg, Canada
Lives: New York City

When was the first time you exhibited your art in public?
I was in a small group show in Winnipeg while I was in art school.

What was that experience like?
I was really overwhelmed by so many things. I had never really traveled before. I was extremely naïve, and I didn't know anything about galleries or the art world in general.

What is the nicest compliment you've received about your work?
What really makes me happy is when children get excited about something they see. Sometimes they are the first to notice something that many adults don't. They can be very intuitive.

What is the most frustrating thing to hear about your work?
The most frustrating thing I hear about my work is that I make too much. I guess because people think about the art market so much, they assume an artist who is productive is motivated by a monetary desire, which is unfortunate. I love to make art and I can't imagine not doing it everyday.

How useful do you think a magazine like *Tokion* can be for an artist?
I think you'd be surprised by how sophisticated and fickle art collectors can be. If anything, I think too much hype can be detrimental to an artist because caring too much about publicity can be a real poison for people.

[from left to right]

Untitled
2006
ink and watercolor on paper
four 13.75 × 10.75 in. drawings, framed

Untitled
2006
ink and watercolor on paper
four 14 × 11 in. drawings, framed

Ceremonies of the Horsemen
2006
ink and watercolor on paper
four 14 × 11 in. drawings, framed

Untitled
2006
ink and watercolor on paper
four 14 × 11 in. drawings, framed

MARGARET
KILGALLEN

Margaret Kilgallen: In the Sweet Bye & Bye
Installation view, REDCAT, Los Angeles.
Collections of the estate of Margaret Kilgallen,
Andrea Bowes, James Elaine, and AG Rosen,
courtesy of the estate of Margaret Kilgallen.
Photo by Scott Groller

OS GEMEOS

Born: São Paulo, Brazil
Live: São Paulo, Brazil

When was the first time you exhibited your art in public?
In the streets of São Paulo in '88, when we started to do graffiti. [The first time] in a gallery was in 2000, in São Paulo also, in a museum called MIS.

What was that experience like?
We've had so many experiences, in the streets of São Paulo and also in the world. What is special about São Paulo is that we always have to pay attention, because you never know what is going to happen. People make their own laws, so you go out and don't know if you'll come back home or not. But you learn a lot from this city, and even with the bad moments, everything is satisfying.

What is one lesson you've learned since that time?
When we started, we didn't have any information about graffiti outside Brazil), like the scene in the U.S. and Europe. This was really great because it made us develop our own way to paint graffiti, since everything we learned, we learned alone, in the streets. Here, we start painting using latex and rollers, and we use spray paint for the outlines, and in the U.S., they only use spray cans. In those days, we didn't have money to buy spray paint, so we used a lot of latex paint, and today we still love and always use that technique.

How would you say your relationship to your work has evolved since that time?
When we started to go more with our own "world" and use more Brazilian influences, we found a way to really express ourselves. It's like you open a window and find another window. Today we know that what we do is something from us, with many influences, but from us.

Untitled
2006
latex on wall
6 feet high

O Dia em que a Andorinha nao voou
2005
mixed media
71 × 55 in.

O Pescador de Ilusoes
2005
mixed media
60 × 45 in.

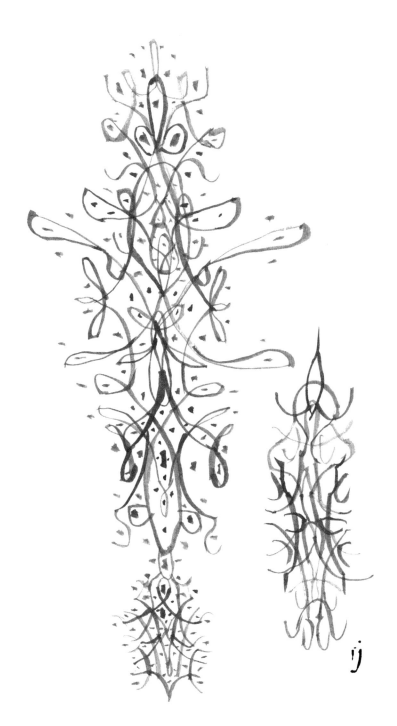

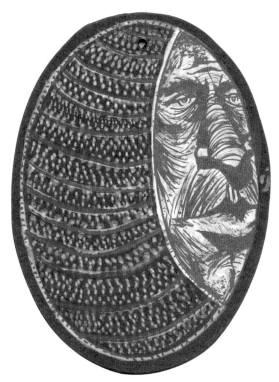

RICH JACOBS

Born: Long Beach, CA
Lives: San Francisco, CA

When was the first time you exhibited your art in public?
Maybe it was Georges Gallery in Los Angeles,
around 1997? Or on the wall much earlier,
I suppose.

What is one lesson you've learned since that time?
I try to look at it like a personal trip through
one's own existence: learning and gathering
useful and/or helpful information all along the
way. My advice to myself is to remember that
things generally go where they are supposed to.

What is the nicest compliment you've received about
your work?
The fact that there are a million things to see
and like out there, but they picked yours . . .
that's crazy, but feels genuinely nice.

If you could change one thing about how you make and
exhibit work, what would it be?
I would be a social worker.

| from left to right |

People on the Wall
2003
acrylic ink on wallpaper
46 × 36 in.

Not Really Tribal More Like Fake Pin Striping
2006
acrylic ink
5 × 11 in.

*Sometimes You Feel Like a Nut—Other Times
You Might Not....*
2005
orange sumi ink over gesso on masonite
5 × 7 in.

SIMONE SHUBUCK

Born: Kuala Lumpur, Malaysia
Lives: New York City

When was the first time you exhibited your art in public?
I did various high school summer art programs from pretty early on and I remember this one performance piece where I danced around all these tree branches set up around a giant puddle.

What was that experience like?
At the time, I thought it was very meaningful and rad, and now I am cringing with embarrassment about what a huge dork I was.

What is one lesson you've learned since that time?
You can't give a fuck about what anyone thinks or it's game over. I also really try to be happy whenever I can manage it.

Do you feel more comfortable in what you do now?
I feel far less comfortable, but I think the stakes get higher all the time and people seem to want to see change in your work to satisfy their own large appetites for more, bigger, and better. On the other hand, continuing to do the same thing endlessly is boring.

What is the nicest compliment you've received about your work?
I got a review recently where the writer was throwing around crazy words like Guston and Twombly. I didn't feel worthy of that.

What is the most frustrating thing to hear about your work?
That it looks like I'm a female Keegan McHargue.

If you could change one thing about how you make and exhibit work, what would it be?
I would use robots more and my own hands less.

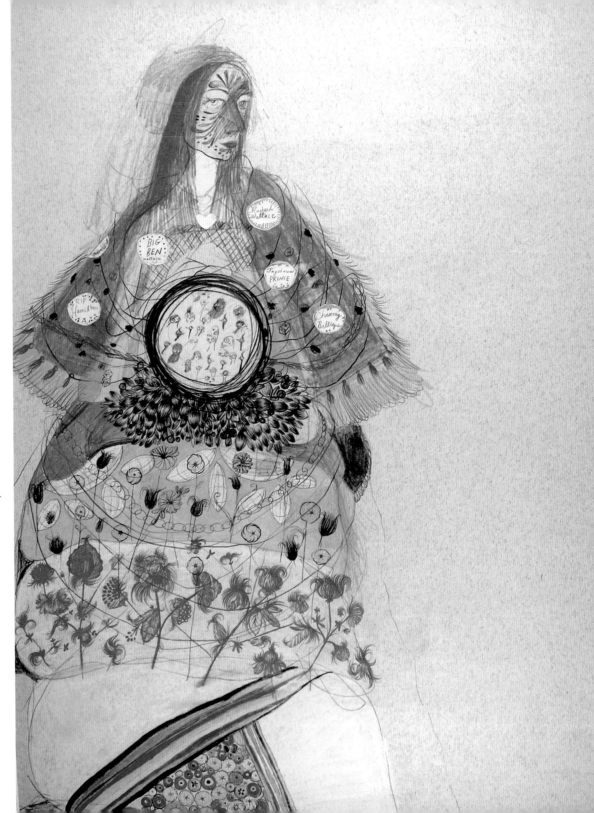

[from left to right]

Pistons Starter
2005
Mixed media
17 × 22 in.

Schiele/Marni Desire Conflict
2005
Mixed media on paper
39 × 28 in.

THOMAS CAMPBELL

Born: Laguna Beach, CA
Lives: Santa Cruz, CA

When was the first time you exhibited your art in public?
When I was twenty I worked for a short time
at a tourist trinket shop in Maui, and one day
when I was working there selling plastic junk, I
met this cool guy named Randy was an artist
and some kind of tomato scientist for Heinz
ketchup in Modesto, in the central California
agricultural area. We became friends and some
time later, after I moved back to the mainland,
Randy helped organize a show for me and some
of my friends at a gallery/coffee shop in the
middle of California. I curated the show, mostly
with skateboarding people: Andy Jenkins, Jeff
Tremaine, Spike Jonze, Todd Swank, maybe Dan
Esterbrook . . . I can't remember the rest–it was
so long ago. That was my first public exhibition,
I'm pretty sure.

What was that experience like?
The experience was pretty mellow. Barely
anyone came to the opening, but a lot of the
artists traveled to the show, so it was nice to
see friends and see their new work.

What is one lesson you've learned since that time?
When exhibiting, the painting you think will
sell first will sell last, and the one you almost
didn't think you were going to put in the
show because you thought it was a bit weak
compared to the others will sell first.

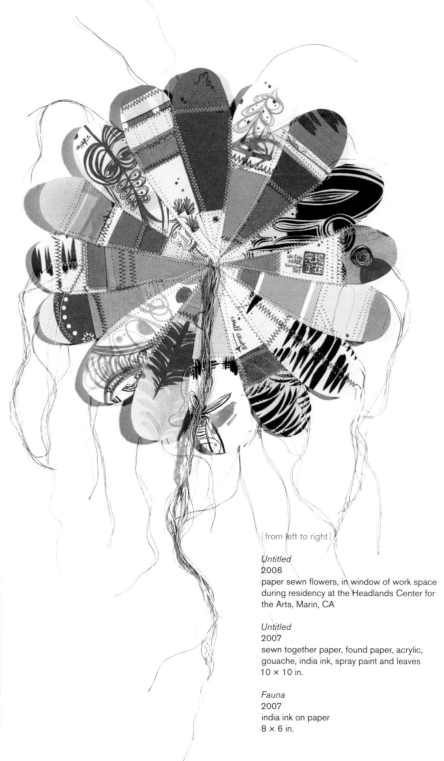

[from left to right]

Untitled
2006
paper sewn flowers, in window of work space
during residency at the Headlands Center for
the Arts, Marin, CA

Untitled
2007
sewn together paper, found paper, acrylic,
gouache, india ink, spray paint and leaves
10 × 10 in.

Fauna
2007
india ink on paper
8 × 6 in.

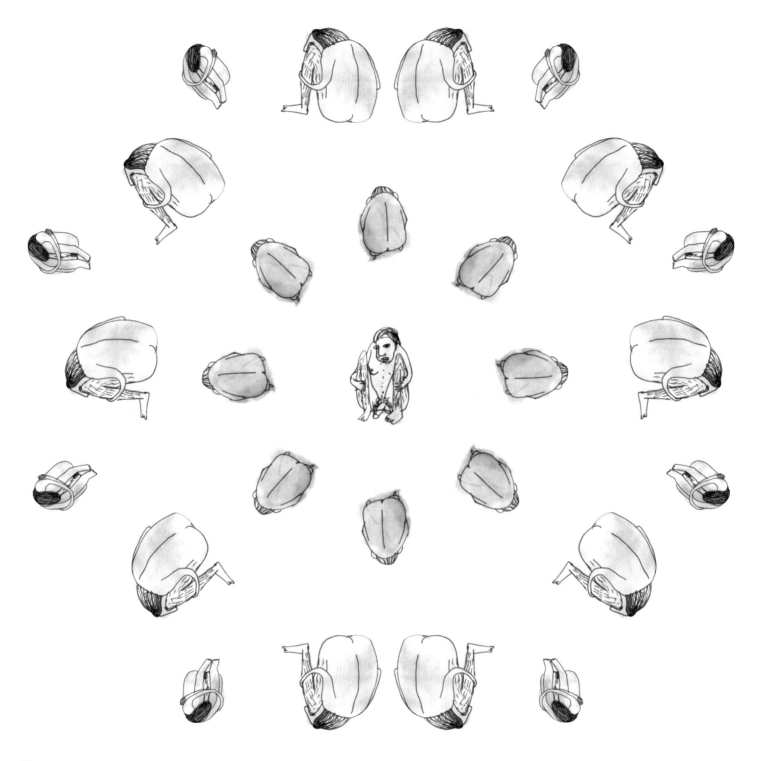

TIFFANY MALAKOOTI

Born: Perth, Australia
Lives: Valencia, CA

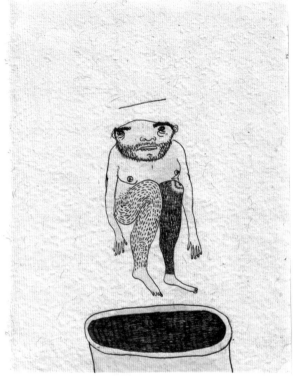

When was the first time you exhibited your art in public?
An exhibition of posters held in Toronto about four years ago called "Tekko."

What was that experience like?
I felt uncomfortable . . . chagrined . . . regretful. There was a lot of attention being given to work I didn't feel great about. I still feel like this when I show stuff today. This book included.

What is one lesson you've learned since that time?
I've learned to say no more often.

What is the nicest compliment you've received about your work?
That it made someone consider their culture in their own work.

What is the most frustrating thing to hear about your work?
Compliments, when I feel they're undeserved or for the wrong reasons.

If you could change one thing about how you make and exhibit work, what would it be?
I would give the work more time.

[from left to right]

Untitled
2006
watercolor and pen
13 × 13 in.

Untitled
2007
pen and digital output
6 × 9 in.

Untitled
2007
pen and digital output
6 × 9 in.

Untitled
2006
pen and digital output
4.5 × 6 in.

TOMOO GOKITA

Born: Tokyo, Japan
Lives: Tokyo, Japan

When was the first time you exhibited your art in public?
When I was in high school, I attached my work
to my body and walked around on the train.

What was that experience like?
I humiliated myself.

How would you say your relationship to your work has
evolved since that time?
I still humiliate myself. I have had that same
feeling since that time.

[from left to right]

Hard Hat Topless
2007
gouache and spray paint on canvas
51 × 76 in.

Orthopedic Surgery
2006
gouache and spray paint on canvas
63.25 × 51 in.

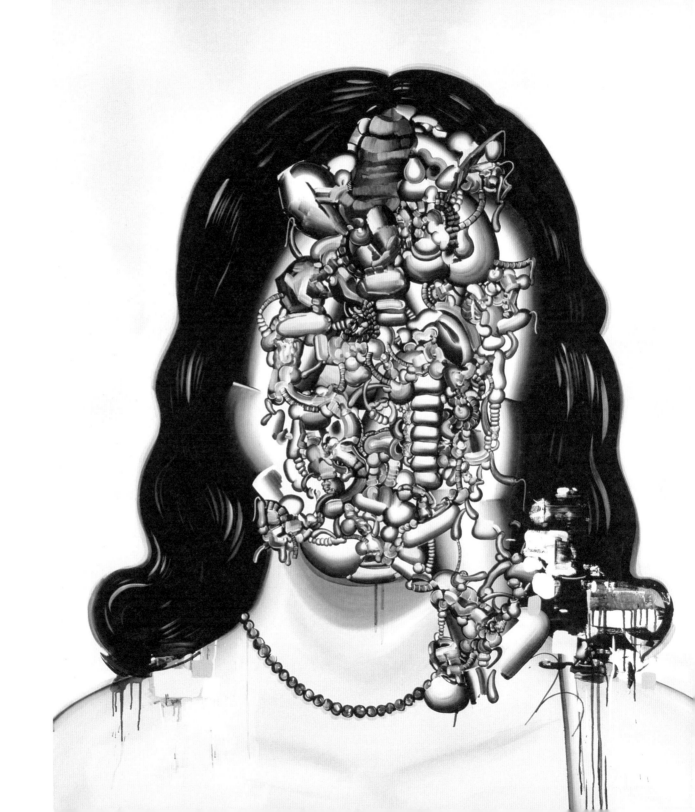

WES LANG

Born: Chatham, NJ
Lives: New York City

When was the first time you exhibited your art in public?
My first public exhibition was at the Limner Gallery in midtown Manhattan. It was a show of portraits of presidents' penises. I did Jimmy Carter. He had peanuts for testicles. Hilarious picture.

What was that experience like?
I had a great time doing the painting, and got a lot of great response to it, but it was strange to put something out in the world for the first time—exhilarating and scary at the same time. I suspect that's a rather natural reaction at first.

How would you say your relationship to your work has evolved since that time?
Now that fear is gone. I learned that it's not that big of a deal, and I can't take myself so seriously. I am very lucky to be doing this for a living, a good one at that. A lot of people would kill for the opportunities I've been given. They are just pictures after all.

JIM DRAIN

DAVID ARON

ARIK ROPER

DEANNE CHEUK

ANNA SEW HOY

DEARRAINDROP

CORY ARCANGEL

BJORN COPELAND

DEVIN FLYNN

DYLAN MARTORELL

BRIAN DEGRAW

ERIKA SOMOGYI

CORNELIUS QUABECK

ASSUME VIVID ASTRO FOCUS

FRIENDS WITH YOU

JEREMY BLAKE

SEBASTIAAN BREMER

HISHAM BHAROOCHA

KEIKO ITAKURA

TIMOTHY MARVEL HULL

PAPER RAD

TAKESHI MURATA

JUDITH SUPINE

SAEKO TAKAGI

RITA ACKERMANN

MIKE PARE

TRACY NAKAYAMA

[from left to right]

Yearbook II
2006
signatures on birch logs
dimensions variable

Soul Girl
2005
ink, watercolor, and colored pencil on paper
18 × 19 in.

Ink Blot 9
2005
ink and colored pencil on paper
14 × 15 in.

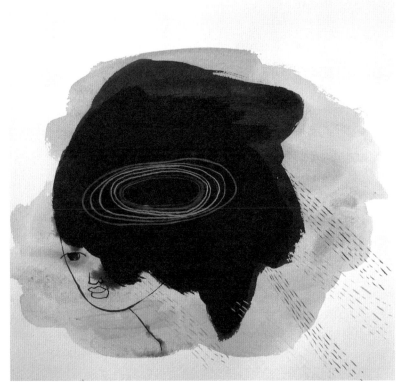

ANNA SEW HOY

Born: Auckland, New Zealand
Lives: Los Angeles, CA

When was the first time you exhibited your art in public?
My first exhibition was probably in 1997, in the gallery at Anthology Film Archives in New York, underneath the screening room. My best friend at this time was a projectionist at Anthology, and I spent most evenings there, watching the experimental cinema program for free, and then drinking vodka in the back office with Jonas Mekas and the other filmmakers. My friend asked me to curate a show in Anthology's Courthouse Gallery. School chums Bella Foster, José León Cerillo, Takuya S., and I made paintings (together) and decided to present them under the moniker Team Easel. We filled the gallery walls with colorful, glittery, goopy, pop paintings and had a party to open the show.

What was that experience like?
I loved organizing the show. I remember that some artists we admired came to look at the show and were confused by "all the glitter," but I didn't care. I was excited that they actually showed up. I enjoyed the social aspect of exhibiting. I was ambitious for my own work, but also aware that showing was a way of forming bonds with other artists and people in general.

What is one lesson you've learned since that time?
This is a practical lesson, and I've been learning it my whole life: how to keep a daily practice. Working daily keeps my ideas flowing, and ensures that my work deepens and progresses, due to looking at it all day and responding to what I see.

How would you say your relationship to your work has evolved?
I know more and more about my work as I make it. I would compare this progression with getting to know someone who will become your best friend.

If you could change one thing about how you make and exhibit work, what would it be?
If I could have anything, I would have a teleporter, as seen in *Star Trek*, so that my sculptures would just materialize in the exhibition space with no preparations, trucks, or crates.

ARIK ROPER

Born: New York City
Lives: New York City

|from left to right|

Matt and Lemmy
2006
watercolor illustration for *Revolver* magazine
8 × 11 in.

Untitled
2005
watercolor and ink illustration for T-shirt graphic
9 × 10 in.

When was the first time you exhibited your art in public?
When I was a kid, I remember teachers and other adults putting up drawings I'd done and asking me to design bulletin boards and brochures. Even then, I'd try to sneak weird or subversive elements into my drawings when possible.

What is one lesson you've learned since that time?
When doing your own art, do what you like to do. Don't alter your art for trends or any other reason that isn't natural. Do what you're into, and it will show.

What is the nicest compliment you've received about your work?
"It's hard to look at."

What is the most frustrating thing to hear about your work?
"It's 'of the moment.'"

How useful do you think a magazine like *Tokion* can be for an artist?
A magazine is more effective than a gallery. It reaches more people. Most people with gallery shows probably hope their show will end up in an art magazine, anyway.

ASSUME VIVID
ASTRO FOCUS

Born: Various
Live: Nomadically

What is the nicest compliment you've received about your work?
A guard during the 2004 Whitney Biennial told us that whenever he would have one of those bad days at work—depressed, sad, or fed up—he would go into our installation and stay there for five minutes or so. He said everything would be different and brighter afterward, as if his energy had shifted focus to a more positive side.

What is the most frustrating thing to hear about your work?
People often forget that this is a collaboration project, and it is annoying to realize that this is so difficult for people to understand. It is very simple, really: AVAF is a collective. One other thing that can be frustrating is when people refer to our over-colored work in a rather superficial way. Can't colors be taken seriously?

If you could change one thing about how you make and exhibit work, what would it be?
To make it accessible to more and more people, regardless of age, sex, race, class, or anything else. The art world is very limiting and self-centered.

How useful do you think a magazine like *Tokion* can be for an artist?
People should find alternative ways of promotion and distribution in order to reach out to a wider variety of people. Magazines serve well in that sense, since they travel easily. But at the same time they don't play videos or music, they don't have odor, and they are not peer-to-peer based. They are sort of dinosaurs ready to be surpassed by some new species yet to come.

Tom Cruising
2005
wallpaper installation
dimensions variable

BJORN COPELAND

Born: Malone, NY
Lives: New York City

When was the first time you exhibited your art in public?
I guess the first stuff I showed in public was in elementary school, you know for conferences and stuff like that.

What was that experience like?
As you can guess from the last answer, my recollections are a bit hazy. In general, I enjoy showing, but am a bit uncomfortable at my own openings.

If you could change one thing about how you make and exhibit work, what would it be?
I wish it was easier sometimes, but who knows if that would make it better. I doubt it.

How useful do you think a magazine like *Tokion* can be for an artist?
Magazines seem to be an effective way to expose people to artists. I'm assuming most have larger circulations than galleries have monthly visitors.

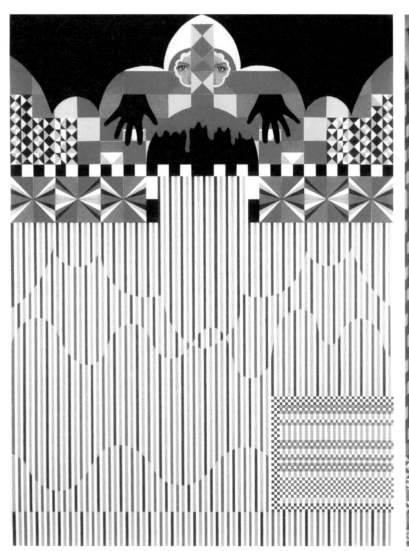

BRIAN DEGRAW

Born: CT
Lives: New York City

When was the first time you exhibited your art in public?
My mom used to have a wall for me in our house when I was about five years old. She would put up all my drawings of turkeys and penguins or whatever I made in school. At some point, I guess I was drawing all over the house, on furniture and things, so my parents painted the walls of my bedroom with chalkboard paint, and I would just go nuts in there. It was like living inside a Cy Twombly painting, but with strange cartoonish characters popping out from behind all the scribble. I have photos of it still.

What is one lesson you've learned since that time?
I used to say yes to every show offer, even if I was feeling uninspired. This is a bad look. Now I understand that I should never show a piece of work that is made solely for the sake of a deadline.

What is the nicest compliment you've received about your work?
"Total garbage."

If you could change one thing about how you make and exhibit work, what would it be?
I would eliminate the concept of the studio visit. I would like to just make detailed proposals for shows, rather than having someone come over and sift through my work. That process gives me anxiety, because oftentimes all my work is in my head, and I don't have concrete evidence of it yet. So a studio visit with Brian DeGraw is more of a tour of the objects in my house . . . couch, movies, a well-organized produce drawer in the fridge, and a note or two to myself taped to the wall. I believe that ought to be enough. Gallerists need to practice the art of energy detection.

[from left to right]

Osama Bin Laden/John Lee Malvo (Series)
2004
graphite on paper
13 × 11 in.

Osama Bin Laden/John Lee Malvo (Series)
2004
graphite on paper
13 × 11 in.

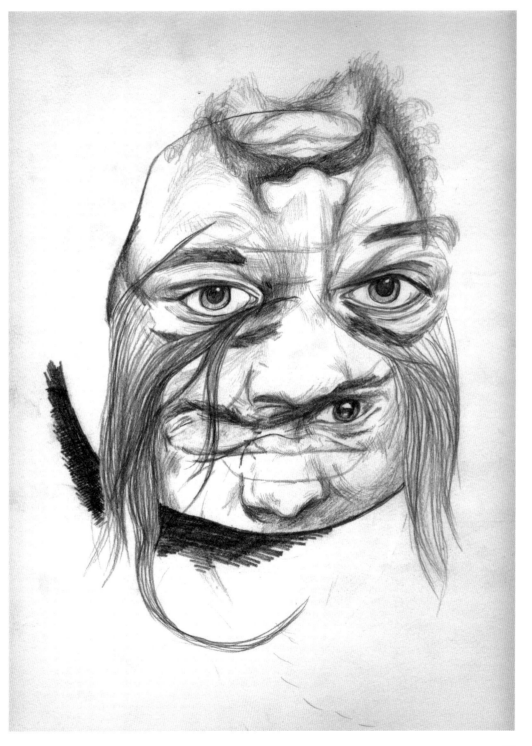

CORNELIUS QUABECK

Born: Wuppertal, Germany
Lives: Duesseldorf, Germany

When was the first time you exhibited your art in public?
I did a show in a friend's empty office in 1998. We printed a real invite (500 copies) and had friends over for beers.

What was that experience like?
I got very excited about having my own invitation card.

What is the nicest compliment you've received about your work?
Nice compliments are not something I look for when I make art, but rather for when I dress sharp.

What is the most frustrating thing to hear about
your work?
To hear nothing.

[from left to right] *Slash*
2005
airbrush and fabric paint on canvas
90.5 × 106.25 in.

Jeff
2005
charcoal and airbrush paint on canvas
90.5 × 102.4 in.

CORY ARCANGEL

Born: Buffalo, NY
Lives: New York City

When was the first time you exhibited your art in public?
My high school had a year-end project show in a hockey rink where the ice had been melted. That's the kind of thing that would only happen in Buffalo, though considering I spent half of my life in hockey rinks growing up, it weirdly makes sense. My dream is still to be in the NHL. No joke.

What was that experience like?
I have no memory of the event except thinking it was cool that my video monitor was where the goalie net would normally be.

What is one lesson you've learned since that time?
I have learned that what you think you want to do isn't always what you want to do. Often I imagine myself doing all this amazing stuff with my spare time (going to museums, writing manifestos, etc., etc.), but then I always end up fucking around on my computer and surfing the web till my eyes bleed.

What is the nicest compliment you've received about your work?
"That's it?!" People are amazed sometimes that my videos are almost nothing. They can't believe I would have the nerve to show so little.

As far as you know, how have most people discovered your work, or what has gotten you the most attention?
Putting my projects online was the best thing I ever did to get attention. All of the other stuff came after.

[from left to right]

Untitled (after Lucier)
2006
digital video still

Every CSNY
2007
ink on paper
8 × 11 in.

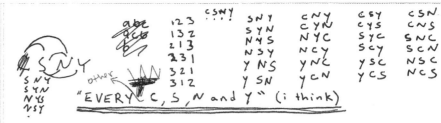

DAVID ARON

Born: Los Angeles, CA
Lives: New York City

When was the first time you exhibited your art in public?
Besides art school in Colorado, the first show I was in was at [the bar] Max Fish. Greg, who still works there, handed out these wooden discs to anyone who wanted to participate. One of the classes I was taking at the time was a portrait class, so I just cut out this portrait of Stalin that was for an assignment, and glued it onto the circle. I painted him because he seemed easy to paint.

What was that experience like?
I was probably really proud of myself, like I'd made it into the city and people would see me as an artist.

What is one lesson you've learned since that time?
I'm still learning that lesson: dissolving pride. It's a sneaky bugger.

How would you say your relationship to your work has evolved since that time?
Before, there was too much want, which equates to false vision, or no vision at all.

What is the nicest compliment you've received about your work?
That the work suggests some kind of heaven.

[from left to right]

Inside the Sun
2006
ink on paper
8.5 × 8 in.

Transcendent Smile
2006
ink on paper
10 × 12 in.

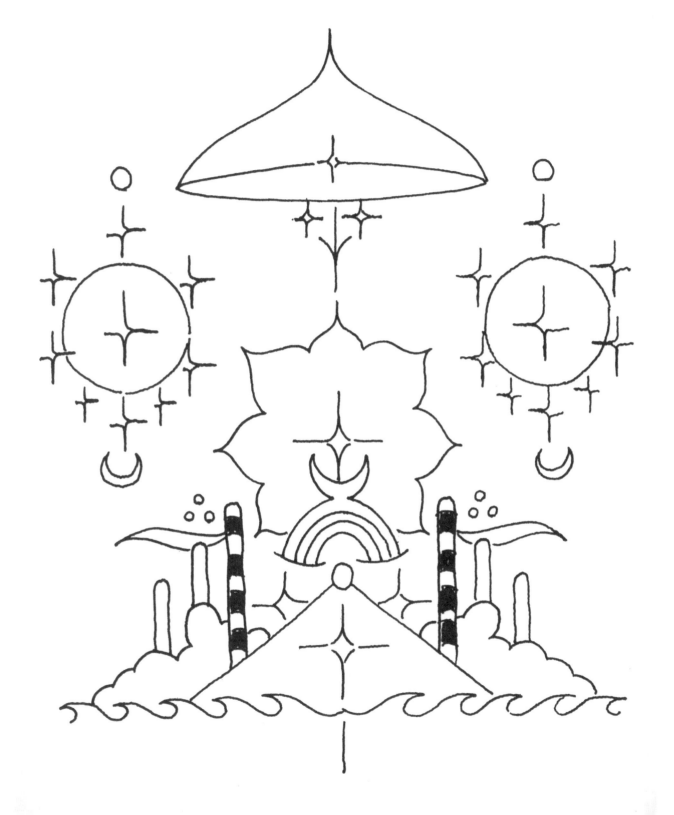

DEANNE CHEUK

Born: Perth, Australia
Lives: New York City

When was the first time you exhibited your art in public?
It was a group show in Perth. I showed some
photos. One was a photo of doll parts. How
embarrassing.

What was that experience like?
It was a charity show, so I felt it was rewarding.

What is one lesson you've learned since that time?
That art is hard to understand. You might like it
at first, and then years later despise it, or you
might love it and everyone else might hate it. I
know that is obvious, but when you're making
it, it is hard to accept.

How would you say your relationship to your work has
evolved since that time?
My work started out as a labor of love until I
started to get paid to do what I love doing.
But even when I was hardly paid anything, it
was still something I knew I wanted to do.

| from left to right |

Untitled
2007
illustration commission for American Rag Cie,
Japan

Untitled
2006
illustration commission for *The Fader* magazine

DEARRAINDROP

Joe Grillo
Born: Meteor City, AZ
Lives: Virginia Beach, VA

Laura Grant
Born: Detroit, MI
Lives: Virginia Beach, VA

Billy Grant
Born: Norfolk, VA
Lives: Virginia Beach, VA

When was the first time you exhibited your art in public?
Probably at Lynn Haven Mall in Virginia Beach in 1991. Joe did a really bad updated super-violent version of Picasso's *Guernica* with cut-up felt, beans, and yarn.

What is one lesson you've learned since that time?
Don't trust anyone, blindly assuming they have your best interest at heart.

What is the nicest compliment you've received about your work?
Weirdest: This really old man came into one of our painting installations and commented that if he was dying in a hospital bed he would not want to be surrounded by our work.

If you could change one thing about how you make and exhibit work, what would it be?
No more fifty-fifty gallery split unless they work really hard for their half.

As far as you know, how have most people discovered your work, or what has gotten you the most attention?
Stupid hype.

[from left to right]

Ray Johnson Chrome Lungs
2005
ink on paper
9 × 12 in.

Iwo Jima Me
2005
mixed media on canvas
20 × 20 in.

Untitled
2006
acrylic and collage on book cover
40 × 30 cm

DEVIN FLYNN

Born: Munich, Germany
Lives: New York City

When was the first time you exhibited your art in public?
I'll keep graffiti out of this, but I will say technically I have been "exhibiting in public" since junior high school. One of the first actual shows I was involved in was the "best of the west" show at the LA art gallery 01, which had a list of hundreds of names on the postcard. A typical bottomless pit of a group show.

What was that experience like?
I was naïve and confident. The opening was a zoo of ambitious monkeys. It was alienating, but that is a satisfying feeling when you are twenty and convinced you are different and misunderstood, etc.

What is one lesson you've learned since that time?
No amount of recognition can improve your work.

Paranoid
2006
video still

Y'all So Stupid
2006
video still

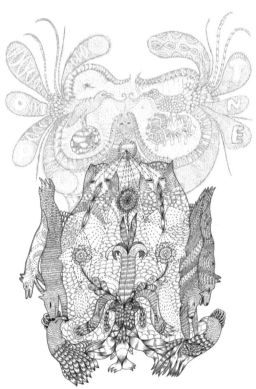

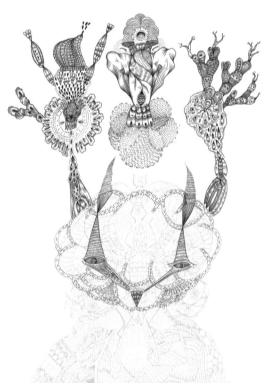

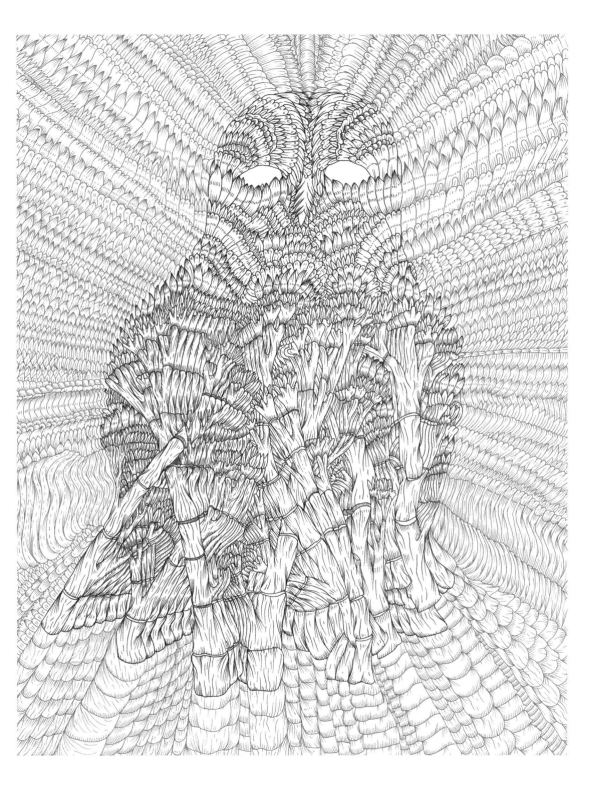

DYLAN MARTORELL

Born: Lanark, Scotland
Lives: Melbourne, Australia

How would you say your relationship to your work has
evolved since you started?
I love printmaking and drawing, but now that art
and music have become my daily life and bread,
there are other pressures involved, especially
with a family. Luckily, I still have the freedom to
pursue projects that I know aren't going to make
any money. I got some automatic spam poetry
e-mailed to me that said, "Mirrors remain feline,
there is a dream but no money." I tentatively took
this as a positive sign. I'm also trying to use the
gallery space these days as a work in progress,
rather than opening the show with the finished
product. I like the idea that creation is taking
place within the gallery, and that the gallery is a
live space rather than a showroom for finished
products.

[from left to right]

AOA
2006
costume and snare drum photograph and
stickers
29.5 × 11.8 in.

Tawny Frogmouth
2005
screen print
23.5 x 27.5 in.

Cicci
2006
screen print
19.7 × 31.5 in.

Lyres
2006
screen print
17.7 × 25.4 in.

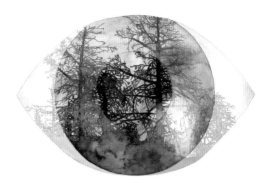

ERIKA SOMOGYI

Born: Suffern, NY
Lives: New York City

When was the first time you exhibited your art in public?
My work was displayed in lots of children's art shows when I was a kid. The shows were mostly in public libraries, but then a watercolor I had made was in a show at the Children's Museum in New York! I was super excited, but never had a chance to go see it. It was a painting of Spike walking down the halls of Degrassi Junior High. She was pregnant.

What was that experience like?
I'm always nervous before an opening of a show. Before one show I had to send my work off a few weeks early to be framed. As the opening date got closer, I had dreams that my watercolors looked muddy and drab. Then, when I saw them again, I was relieved to find them bright and clear. I still have that problem: when my work is far from me, my memory of it is so cloudy.

What is the most frustrating thing to hear about your work?
"Cool . . . drugged out teenagers from the '70s."
Or, "Did you sell anything?"

If you could change one thing about how you make and exhibit work, what would it be?
I would like to be able to look at my older art while making new work.

Light Eyes
2007
watercolor on paper
diptych
11 × 14 in. each

Past, Present, Future
2007
watercolor and gouache on paper
22 × 26 in.

Just Close Your Eyes
2006
watercolor and gouache on paper
15 × 22 in.

FRIENDS WITH YOU

Arturo Sandoval
Born: Havana, Cuba
Lives: Miami, FL

When was the first time you exhibited your art in public?
I was doing full installations in high school. They would be interactive, and sometimes dangerous.

What was that experience like?
I never was scared to show what I had inside. No matter if it was good or bad, I always just had to put it out there, kind of like a signal to anyone who felt the same way.

What is one lesson you've learned since that time?
I've learned that life is precious, and that my contribution and responsibility to my life and the world around me can be more significant than I ever had thought in that moment. I learned more about love and how to treat people. And I keep learning.

Do you have a peer network that supports you in your work?
Of course. Tury Sandoval is one. And I am finding so many supporters all over the world, and it keeps increasing. It's kind of like this network of people who have a spiritual mission on this world to spread empowerment and collectively organize to make things happen and to change the world as it gets easier and easier to do with new information systems.

What is the most frustrating thing to hear about your work?
Um, nothing. I like the good and bad things I hear. It helps always to formulate a solution or a resolve.

Victory
2006
digital media

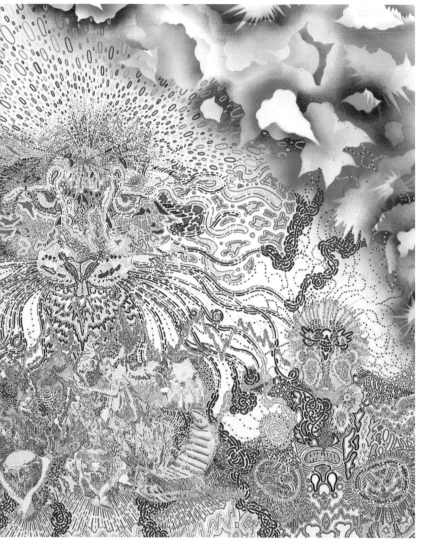

[from left to right]
Once The Incision Is Made
2006
glitter glue, acrylic, oil-based paint, and paper
on wood panel
48 × 60 in.

Moon Oar Sunrise
2005
collage and ink on paper
8 × 10 in.

Le Vieux Soulard et Sa Femme
2007
collage on paper
7 × 9.5 in.

HISHAM AKIRA BHAROOCHA

Born: Niigata, Japan
Lives: New York City

What is one lesson you've learned since you started?
There are so, so, so many lessons I've learned, but maybe the most important one is to keep making work that comes from your heart, not from your mind. Living in New York, it's easy to get stuck in your head about what is the best thing to do in order to "make it" as an artist. You start to think you need to make work by New York standards, make work that speaks in the language the audience is interested in at the moment and all that nonsense. We all feel it. I sure as hell did. The competition is so heavy here, but I realized it's only heavy if I make it an issue for myself. I now concentrate on actually making work, not where it's going to be shown, or if it's valid in the context of art history or New York art standards. I can only make what I feel inspired to make. It's as simple as that.

How would you say your relationship to your work has evolved since that time?
I'd say my work has become less self-conscious over the years. It finally feels like I have a language of my own that I can sample from, depending on the project I'm working on. I am excited to know that the boundaries of my work, or anyone's creation, are limitless.

What is the nicest compliment you've received about your work?
That it emanates peace and light.

How useful do you think a magazine like *Tokion* can be for an artist?
One thing I try to keep in mind is that you don't want your art to seem like an illustration to a story, or an advertisement, unless that's what it's being used for and you've agreed to that being the context of how it's seen. You want people to take your work seriously. If the work has conviction and integrity, the work will stand on its own, no matter where it's published. I actually got my last solo exhibition because a curator in Europe started to see my work published in magazines. It was just the starting point of him getting interested, but it was a point of departure.

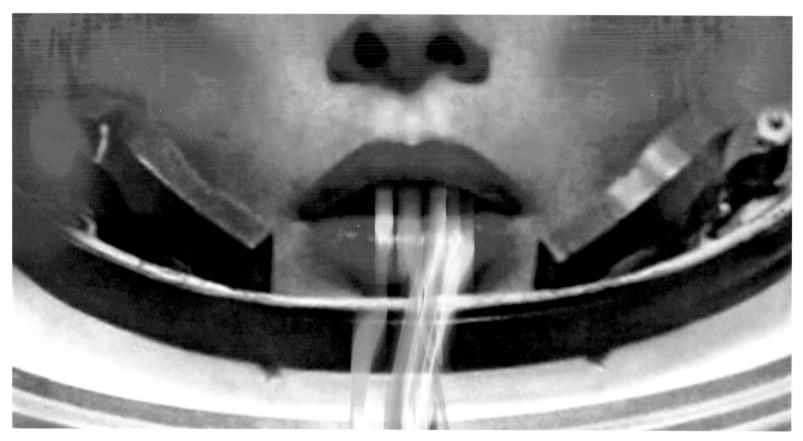

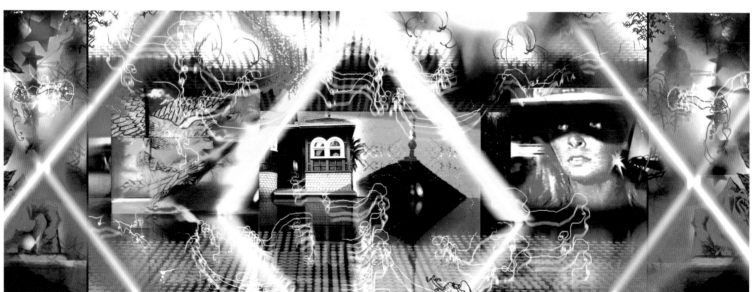

JEREMY BLAKE

Born: Fort Sill, OK

When was the first time you exhibited your art in public?
I think it was the time when I opened my
raincoat and dropped my drawers in front of
the statues of nude Roman babes at the Met
and yelled, "Hey all you foxy ladies! Expose
yourselves to art!" I was only three years old.

What was that experience like?
Well, the museum guards were freaked because
they had never seen a three-year-old with adult-
size genitals before.

What is one lesson you've learned since that time?
People crave meaning very badly. They crave
"the new" aesthetically, but then they freak out
a little when you actually deliver.

How would you say your relationship to your work has
evolved since that time?
I am more and more comfortable with what I do,
and less and less comfortable with the world
around me.

What is the nicest compliment you've received about
your work?
There was that time, about ten years ago now,
that Sharon Stone came through the Centre
Pompidou and sat down next to me and told me
that *Angel Dust*, my first experimental DVD, had
"completely mastered space, time, and matter."

Then she told my girlfriend, Theresa, that she
was beautiful. I think that is the nicest anyone
has been in a single afternoon, and I don't really
care if it was sincere or not, or even if what she
was saying made any sense.

What is the most frustrating thing to hear about your
work?
If people are talking at all, I'm happy. That's what
art is for, to get a diversity of opinion flowing.

{from left to right}

Reading Ossie Clark
2004
video still

Glitterbest
2007
video still

Witch's Cap
2004
video still

[from left to right]

Sad Dad
2007
collaged materials
10 × 11 in.

We Hid Behind the Rocks and Waited
2007
collaged materials
10 × 12 in.

JIM DRAIN

Born: Cleveland, OH
Lives: Miami, FL

When was the first time you exhibited your art in public?
In 1983, my school drawing became the March
illustration for an international animal rights
calendar. My picture was taken for the school
paper with my teacher, Mrs. Gasser. I think I was
waiting for a cash prize. It felt kind of awesome
and disappointing at the same time.

What is one lesson you've learned since that time?
I think I learned that rewards are arbitrary.

How would you say your relationship to your work has
evolved since that time?
I don't think I look to my work as a way to solve
problems, but more to help define questions I
cannot otherwise name.

If you could change one thing about how you make and
exhibit work, what would it be?
I wish the work could be all things: a sound,
a vaccine, a hammer, a way to see ghosts,
something that reveals mystical truths. I think it
is more a matter of being critical without being
judgmental, of just letting the work be what it is.

How useful do you think a magazine like *Tokion* can be for
an artist?
Try buying something from a Sears catalog—it
always looks different from the picture.

JUDITH SUPINE

Born: Portsmouth, VA
Lives: New York City

When was the first time you exhibited your art in public?
A few years ago, I decided I was going to paste a poster on an abandoned gas station in Richmond, Virginia.

What was that experience like?
It was five a.m., and I was candy flipping, so I started getting supper paranoid. I went back the next day and realized I had pasted the poster with the image facing the wall.

What is one lesson you've learned since that time?
I learned to concentrate on the obvious.

How would you say your relationship to your work has evolved since that time?
I really love the artist lifestyle: wake up late, drink tea, glue some pieces of paper together.

KEIKO ITAKURA

Born: Tokyo, Japan
Lives: Tokyo, Japan

When was the first time you exhibited your art in public?
It was in kindergarten.

What was that experience like?
I could easily imagine rainbow-colored butterflies
and play with them, and I could listen to any
imaginary music. My immature brain allowed me
to go to such extremes, and I couldn't distinguish
what was real and what was not. I cherish
and hold in high esteem those fragile, pure
experiences.

What is one lesson you've learned since that time?
Keep holding exhibits. I've become a more
severe critic of myself and also keep a certain
objective distance between myself and my art,
in order to understand myself more critically.

If you could change one thing about how you make and
exhibit work, what would it be?
The colors.

[from left to right]

K
2003
pen and paper
117 × 82.6 in.

My Poodle
2006
pen and paper
70.8 × 78.7 in.

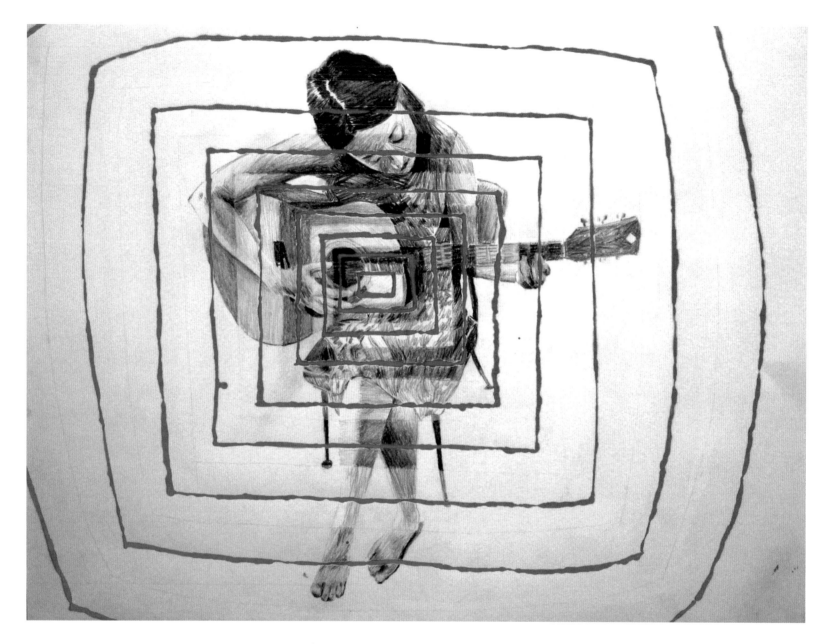

MIKE PARÉ

Born: Northern California
Lives: New York City

When was the first time you exhibited your art in public?
It was in a dumpy storefront gallery run by my friend Miguel Strong.

What was that experience like?
It was great. I hung up dozens of small paintings and drawings. It was satisfying to hang all the work up at once.

What is one lesson you've learned since that time?
It's good to edit. There is no need to show everything.

How would you say your relationship to your work has evolved since that time?
It's boring to make the same thing twice. I think over the years I've learned to trust my intuition

more, and to focus on one piece of work at a time.

How useful do you think a magazine like *Tokion* can be for an artist?

I think it's probably more important for the types of artists who can reach people through mass media like film or music. Artists who sell their individual artworks (or want to) are different from those who make things that can be mass-produced and consumed. Does a magazine help me sell artwork? Probably not.

{ from left to right }

Guitar Lesson
2006
graphite and egg tempera on paper
30 × 22 in.

Everywhere
2006
graphite on paper
22 × 30 in.

Reverbs
2004
graphite and tempera on paper
22 × 30 in.

PAPER RAD

Jacob and Jessica Cioccl, Ben Jones
Born: Pittsburgh, PA, and Lexington, KY
Lives: Pittsburgh, PA, and Providence, RI

When was the first time you exhibited your art in public?
We got together a bunch of new Xeroxed "books" we made—a "body of work," if you will—and had fun handing out our stuff for free to weird or interesting people we saw. We had made a bunch of new stuff and were psyched to encounter new people and found the whole idea exciting, yet funny and silly at the same time.

What is the nicest compliment you've received about your work?
"You are looking very colorful today."

What is the most frustrating thing to hear about your work?
That it's just about '80s nostalgia.

If you could change one thing about how you make and exhibit work, what would it be?
You know: the whole money/artworld/fashion/exclusive/fake-ass/careerist/corrupt/ego-based/superficial/pretentious/meaningless/mean/classist/greed thing.

[from left to right]

The Fake Sunglasses Test
2007
DVD still

USAISAMONSTER
2006
Adobe Illustrator file
size variable

RITA ACKERMANN

Born: Budapest, Hungary
Lives: New York City

When was the first time you exhibited your art in public?
When I was in elementary school, we had a
school district drawing contest and the jury
exhibited the drawings of the finalists.

What was that experience like?
It was very rewarding, because my parents were
proud of me, and I also won acceptance to
an after-school art workshop for the "specially
gifted."

What is one lesson you've learned since that time?
That winning is a great thing but it doesn't
happen all the time.

[from left to right]

If I Was a Maid, Can I Clean Your Flat?
1994
acrylic and pencil on canvas
106 × 54 in.

World War III Around My Skull
1997
acrylic and ballpoint pen on linen, oil varnished
54 × 55 in.

SAEKO TAKAGI

Born: Kyoto, Japan
Lives: Kyoto, Japan

When was the first time you exhibited your art in public?
When I was twenty years old, I won the Showa Shell Contemporary Art Award, so I exhibited my painting at their exhibition.

What was that experience like?
I was pleased for many people to see my painting. It gave me the possibility that I could go on as a professional painter.

What is the nicest compliment you've received about your work?
Somebody once said he felt light shining from my work.

If you could change one thing about how you make and exhibit work, what would it be?
I would like to show my work in spaces other than white cubes.

[from left to right]

Usual Experiences
2007
acrylic and resin on canvas
45.75 × 45.75 in.

Slow Killer
2007
acrylic on canvas
35.5 × 35.5 in.

Zert Tree/Still Steaming Tree 02
2007
acrylic and resin on canvas
46 × 46 in.

SEBASTIAAN BREMER

Born: Amsterdam, the Netherlands
Lives: New York City

When was the first time you exhibited your art in public?
In an open studio program I attended in The Hague, around 1991.

What was that experience like?
It was great—I made these enormous self-portraits, and they were a bit heavy-handed. A student navigating the stairs at night saw them from the corner of her eye, not realizing they were paintings, and fell off the stairs. No injuries, but I guess it made an impression.

What is the nicest compliment you've received about your work?
Seeing people look at my work, and seeing them stay.

What is the most frustrating thing to hear about your work?
That it doesn't reproduce well—that it's not the same as seeing it in front of you.

If you could change one thing about how you make and exhibit work, what would it be?
A *Mission Impossible* system of pulleys, to make me fly over my pieces without having to move them about much. Otherwise, all is fine.

[from left to right]

Poppy
2002
inks on c-print
30 × 40 in.

Superman
2006
inks on c-print
73 × 49.25 in.

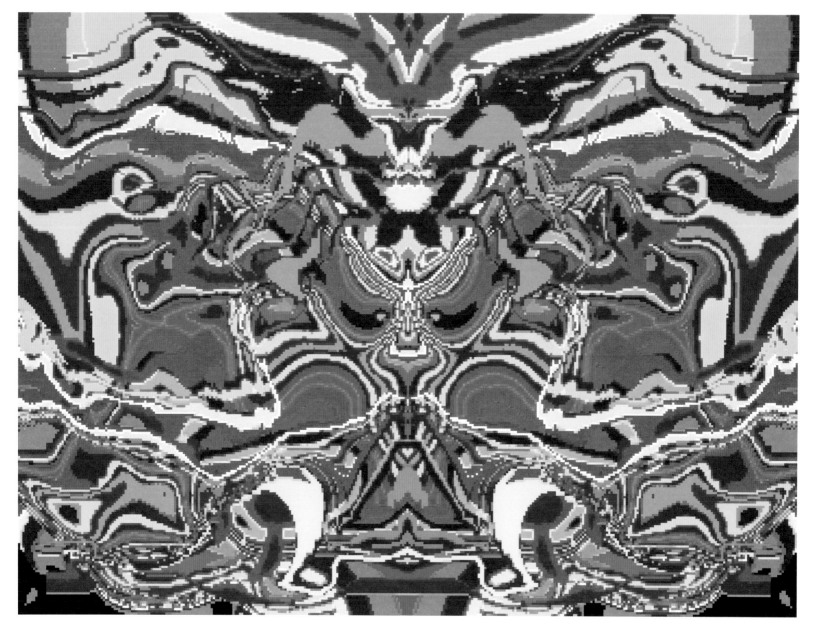

TAKESHI MURATA

Born: Chicago, IL
Lives: Woodstock, NY

When was the first time you exhibited your art in public?
At my friends' homemade art shows.

What is one lesson you've learned since that time?
To make my videos for my friends. When I've made them for other reasons, they come out pretty bad.

What is the nicest compliment you've received about your work?
"I saw my grandmother's ghost in your video."

What is the most frustrating thing to hear about your work?
"Oh, that was yours?"

If you could change one thing about how you make and exhibit work, what would it be?
I would have a WIFI-enabled van.

Cone Eater
2004
four minute video projection with soundtrack by
Robert Beatty

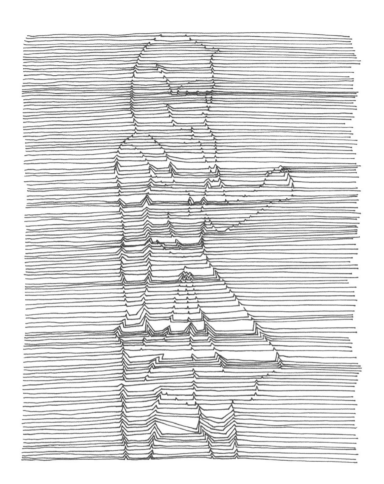

TIMOTHY MARVEL HULL

Born: New York City
Lives: New York City

When was the first time you exhibited your art in public?
I first exhibited in a small bar called Mayday in Florence, Italy, in 2001. It was a photography show. I also showed that year at a restaurant called the Backyard Grill in the sleepy village of Warwick, New York.

What was that experience like?
Exhibiting work in a non-gallery space is sometimes very liberating. People actually tend to look at the work for longer periods of time while they are sitting down, enjoying a meal or a drink. Galleries should take a cue from this and start serving refreshments and having comfortable chairs for viewing works.

What is one lesson you've learned since that time?
The practical lesson I've learned is that people don't really buy art in a non-gallery setting. I've also learned that proper framing is important, and less is more (in everything).

What is the nicest compliment you've received about your work?
Someone (or a few people) said it made them "uncomfortable," and I thought that was a suitable adjective at the time.

What is the most frustrating thing to hear about your work?
I used to hate "whimsical." Now, I don't mind it so much. What's so wrong with a little whimsy?

[from left to right]

*Somewhere Between the Real
and the Miraculous*
2006
graphite on paper
9 × 12 in.

*The Particular Movements of
Tutankhamun*
2007
gel pen on paper
8.5 × 11 in.

*Katherine Mansfield and the
Difficulties of Reality and Dying
of Consumption*
2006
oil on canvas
30 × 42 in.

TRACY NAKAYAMA

Born: Oahu, HI
Lives: Los Angeles, CA

When was the first time you exhibited your art in public?
It was in the seventh grade, when I drew Garfield on my friend's Trapper Keeper.

What was that experience like?
The Trapper Keeper was passed around the classroom, so I was terrified about being made fun of or getting busted by the teacher, but it ended up being a success because my classmates all thought it was cool. I was a bit overwhelmed by all the requests to draw Garfield on backpacks and notebooks, and only later on did I begin to negotiate deals for Hello Kitty erasers and pencils.

What is one lesson you've learned since that time?
I learned to get the pencils and erasers before doing the work. Also, some kid drew a big penis on my Garfield head, making it look like a cock and balls, which really bummed me out. So in the end I had to learn not to be so sensitive about the work once it had left my hands.

How do you discover most artists you like?
Record stores are a great place to find out about art. Just flipping through the Sonic Youth section is one of the best lessons a young person can learn about contemporary art.

[from left to right]

The Seeker
2006
ink and collage on paper
10 × 13 in.

God's Eye
2006
Ink on paper
26 × 40 in.

Valerie
2006
ink on paper
10 × 13 in.